God's Love:

Extravagant Evidence

From Missteps to a Missionary

Book 1

CarolAnn North

ISBN 978-1-63844-908-9 (paperback)
ISBN 978-1-63844-909-6 (digital)

Christian Faith Publishing
832 Park Avenue
Meadville, PA 16335
www.christianfaithpublishing.com

Printed in the United States of America

O God, thou art My God; early will I seek thee: My soul thirsteth for thee, my flesh longeth for thee In a dry and thirsty land, where no water is; to see thy power and thy glory, So as I have seen thee in the sanctuary. Psalm 63:1-2— King James Version

Contents

Excerpts from God's Love: Extravagant Evidence

[Book One]

From *Hungary Heals*—1

This email requesting a hold on our commitment needed my immediate attention. At the risk of behaving like an "ugly American," I tried to gently persuade my Hungarian colleagues not to change the plans for my arrival in Hungary. I communicated to them how much faith I had in God to turn this situation into a blessing for some students there in Hungary. I did not want to alienate myself with them. I spoke to Maria Elgut and perhaps she spoke with them to seek a better alternative than a year's postponement. For a moment I feared that the Hungarian colleagues would just move on from my issues and go forward with their request. After all, what could I do if they simply could not honor my request? In an act of compassion, I believe, not only did they keep the reservation in place, but also because of a medical emergency with my health, I requested respectfully that they even change my departure date to 48 hours later than the original date. Little do they know, even now, that they have made a lifetime friend in me. As my life unfolds, I will not forget their many acts of kindness toward me. They honored all of my requests. This story continues.

From *Particular Pain*—1

One day I sat on a park bench in New York City and watched the children and families stroll by with ice cream cones, some on bicycles, some pet walking, some on roller skates, some bouncing balls, and others just running freely and I felt such a rush of love for them. I became captivated at their beauty, imagining their stories as families. I wondered if I had held marriage and the family in such high esteem and believed so fiercely that love belonged to me—that I possibly created an idol. I confess that over a period of years, I asked God why I felt disillusioned emotionally toward his love, even though intellectually, I knew God's love preserved my life. Nonetheless, this thought caused me a particular kind of pain. Perhaps unrequited love with another interfered with my immersion into God's love. In spite of this particular pain, I embraced the truth that God's love brings healing, deliverance, wisdom, safety, and security. I believe that God's perfect love remains constant throughout our human growth and development experiences. I suspect that I am not alone in this thought pattern and declaration.

Kind Keisha

I returned to the USA from Chiang Mai, Thailand in May 2017. Again, I did not want to return home so soon. When I serve on the mission field, I feel like a giant—like an eagle soaring high above the earth. Soaring with such a strong sense of direction, purpose and fulfillment. Sometimes when I return home to the good old USA from the mission field abroad, I feel less like an eagle and more like a canary. I sense that I am caged and flitting about in a not large enough space; and, I am singing for my supper, chirping to entertain myself, longing for the opened cage door so that I can be free again. I wish that I didn't feel that way.

Acknowledgements

For Mother and Daddy
You never gave up on me!

For my beloved siblings
Harold, Ken and Deb
You love me unconditionally!

For my bonus family members
The Campbells
You inspired me to achieve the highest goals!

For my beloved spiritual sons and daughters
and a host of devoted friends
You motivate me to provide a good example and to press on!.

For my secondary, college, university, and seminary teachers/professors
You inspired my reading, thinking and writing skills!

For my multiple ministry leaders and church families
You pray, love, equip, and care for me even now!

For my voice teachers
You invested in my singing career!

For the missionaries worldwide
You accept me graciously as your own!

For my students in the USA and internationally

CAROLANN NORTH

You taught me more than you know!

For my students at Minimum Security at Lorton prison
You believed in me as a woman of God!

For my enemies
You challenge me to do God's will!

Introduction

What do I want to achieve with the telling of this transformation story?

I pray that some dear soul seeking fulfillment in love will find perfect love in the Creator, Redeemer and Sustainer of life. God's perfect love transformed my life from an embittered, frustrated and unfulfilled state to one of a peaceful acceptance of my purpose. My transformation occurred after I totally surrendered my will to God's will. I seemed to have had an "out of body" experience as I witnessed the melting of my heart and how God filled it with his perfect love. I discovered that my missteps neither defined nor limited God's plan for my Joshua 1:8 good success. In this way, I experienced—from the heavens—an extreme makeover. I am a woman transformed from being selfish, angry, embittered, unfulfilled to a woman whose heart now abounds with love—God's perfect love—that I freely pour into the lives of others. I am a witness that you can live a brand new YOU life and live it NOW.

The Back Story

One bright, sunny day in May 1977, in my comfortable New York City [NYC] apartment, I became introspective. I sat on my deep cushioned, colorful sofa examining the multi-colored threads of the cushions. I loved the tightly woven threads and the patterns they formed. My life seemed multi-colored to me if I thought carefully about my professional desires. I sensed that I had needs that keep going unmet. As I continued running my fingertips across the texture of my sofa, examining the patterns there, I sensed that my life felt like the pattern in the sofa except unlike these tightly woven threads, my life's threads were flapping and disconnected. Tightly woven, all connected, threads on my sofa cushion reminded me of how I wanted my life's purpose to become visible to me in a tightly woven and connected pattern that I could follow. I reflected upon my deepest longing—to witness a radical change in my life and to follow a more productive and fulfilling path. With a will of steel, I pursued with absolute determination, a career in theater arts in NYC. I simply wanted to star on Broadway, sign a recording contract, and read stellar performance reviews. After several years of this lifestyle, I cringed at the attitude I developed. I pushed back from my original plans. I now resisted the long, winding road to success in show business—it became a road littered with my self-serving, angry, demanding behavior toward those I loved. I frowned upon my self-centeredness and how it manifested in striking out at my beloved fiance. I verbally assaulted others with my caustic tongue. I felt disgusted with how I continued along a path of counterproductive behavior. I bowed in humble submission to God's mercy in gratitude that I had not destroyed myself in my desire for stardom.

Because I grew up singing hymns and gospel music—attending church all day every Sunday—and watching my parents cultivate in my siblings and me the Judeo-Christian ethics and biblical principles, I finally yielded to the gnawing in my soul. I no longer ignored my daddy's prayers and my mom's wisdom. As I rocked back and forth on those deep sofa cushions—staring at my hands—wrestling with my thoughts, I began to huddle with God. I now wanted the God of my father and mother to become my God. I needed to test the truth of God's word that states how God will give one the desires of his or her heart. Would God really give me the desires of my heart? I wanted to testify that the scriptures remain viable in the 20th century and beyond. Suddenly resolved, I presented my entire life before God and humbly bowed in submission with this thought: God do with my life whatever you choose. I was done with doing things my way, exercising my will, and ignoring God's word. From 1970 to 1977, I stumbled through enough missteps in my life that I nearly reached a path of no return. Perhaps I might have physically been alive, but spiritual death gnawed at me. My dreams escaped me, my professional success failed me, and my lack of self-worth drained me. I stood in the middle of my living room in my well-lit 15th floor apartment and nursed an acute despondency. I spent several days lingering upon the bright, blue sky—thoroughly disgusted with how little I had achieved since receiving my Bachelor's degree in 1969. My parents reminded me of their hopes for my good success. They continued to pray, counsel and love me unconditionally, but they struggled to mask their critical concerns for my holistic health.

From 1973 to 1977, I abandoned my life with God. I explored my own interests, hopes, and adventures—all of them flying in the face of my parents' expectations—and perhaps even reality. Pursuing a singing and acting career in New York City is not for the faint of heart. As a sensitive soul, I let the frustration get to me—I hated pounding the pavement seeking auditions and banging on closed doors of directors and agencies. In my pursuit of a recording contract and an offer to appear in a musical or drama, I discovered you must attract the attention of agents, directors, composers, and even other artists to get your talent noticed and even affirmed. In connecting with others, you hope to become cast in a show. I did get parts in several shows but they were not on Broadway. Perhaps I let impatience take over. Why did I think that it would be easy? I found some success with DC Black Repertory Theater in Washington, DC. Perhaps I should have remained with that ensemble and learned more about the industry. During this time of reckless abandonment, which according to the scriptures—identifies one as in a backslidden state—I found myself disillusioned with God. Where was God's perfect love for me? What caused me to resist God's way? I erroneously concluded that God should agree with my plan. I wanted my way.

When I reached my 30th birthday, I decided that New York, theater, musical comedy, recording contracts and the like were not for me. Becoming self absorbed felt ugly on the inside. I did not like the woman that I became. I concentrated too much on myself—how boring! Without question, I accepted that God's love for me manifested in extravagant evidence. Petra Garissi Sakarian is in the extravagant evidence gift box from God to me. Petra taught me voice lessons 3 times a week at a nominal fee. When I began to pay rent in NYC, I no longer had a budget for my voice lessons. Petra shared that she had such confidence in my voice that she would teach me for love. This precious woman from Sicily encountered this wide-eyed, southern country girl, from Texas who had hopes for a musical life in NYC, and she invested hundreds of hours in keeping my voice healthy. No dollar amount would ever satisfy Petra's investment in cultivating my 3-octave range, mezzo soprano voice. After some years, I lost contact with Petra. I continued to follow the voice preparation she taught me and sang in multiple other venues. I now yearned to reconnect with Petra so that she could witness the return on her investment in my vocal capacity. I never found her again. Perhaps her daughter and grandchildren will come across this book and allow me to celebrate our beloved Petra. Petra's unusual investment in my voice and her confidence that I had a voice that needed to be heard kept me not only in New York City for several years but continuing to both sing and write music even as of the writing of this book. Though I joined several repertory groups for study purposes, I eventually became distracted by the rigors of show business that dimmed the beauty of the art that I cherished. What bothered me revolved around the "me/my" factors—my figure, my hair, my skin, my talent, my needs, my longings, my awards, my audience, my interests—all prioritized over other things in life that began to interest me far more. I accepted that my soul longed for something bigger than just my will. I hungered for the privilege of giving to make the lives of others richer and rewarding.

In this book, you will find chapters that share the extravagant evidence of God's perfect love engrafted in my heart. I learned from joyful and celebratory moments as well as agonizing and humiliating moments. You might find duplication of some information as you read through or skip chapters. My zeal may exceed wisdom in the rush to share my story. I appreciate in advance your willingness to both read and share this book.

The Forward Story

As my life has progressed from the days of theater and what I learned from them, the days of social activism and what I learned from them, the days of teaching and what I learned from them, and the days of missionary life and ministry and what I learned from them, you will find how all of these experiences matured me as a woman. You will find in chapters an account of what God generously did in my lived experiences that caused me to not only experience God's perfect love, but also to witness the extravagant evidence of that same love. In just a few more paragraphs, I want to share with you how I finally had the courage to sit quietly and pen the story of my radical transformation.

In 2019, I sat in my well lighted, comfortable, colorful flat in a village named Törökszentmiklós, Hungary in eastern Europe. With the sunlight glowing on my desk, I reflected upon the life that I have lived for the past 70 years. On Friday, March 13, 2020, I received a telephone call that stated the world now faced a global pandemic. I understood that our school would close and not likely reopen before the June closing. I was advised to prepare to return to my country and make my decision within an hour. I found that my active and engaging life as a teacher at the Kolcsey Ferenc Primary School had come to a screeching halt. How could this happen? Nonetheless, I chose to remain in Hungary from March 13th to June 15th 2020. I decided that this global pandemic opened the way for me to sit, ponder, meditate, contemplate, reflect, observe and clear my head as I determined to write my story for the benefit of others. I told my Headmaster, Zoli, and Lead Teacher, Kati, that if the world was coming to an end, I would be right there with my newly formed Hungarian family. I had no idea that the global pandemic would allow me a safe harbor, a beautiful landscape, and a protected environment in which to sit from March to June 2020 and author my story. My testimony points to the extravagant evidence of God's perfect love in my life that allowed me to visit nearly every continent in the world. It tells of how God's love in spite of my deep longing for love, romance, marriage and the family ushered me into the lives of the most adorable school children in three different regions of the world. These delightful children treated me like a rock star.

My Hungarian colleagues shared the warmest and most delightful hospitality. At one point I wondered if I were in my last year of life. Good treatment amazes me. I know how to give plenty of it. I love to treat others as if they are the most special people in the world. I, however, struggle when someone makes a big fuss over me. God made the biggest fuss of all over me. God loved me through my ugliest self. He wrapped me in those gentle arms of safety, protected me from my insecurities, and taught me how to freely love, forgive and receive others as my brothers and sisters. In this way, I moved to a healthy appreciation for race relations—considering the gorgeous possibilities of getting along with one another. Only God did this for me. I know because I tried many other ways to become a better human. They failed me.

In this book, you will read how I learned tough lessons of love and acceptance even in the face of professional humiliation inflamed by racial bigotry. I also learned powerful lessons about idolatry. I suspect that I made idols of the institution of marriage and my personal desire for romantic love and a prosperous family. Please know, I learned that when you want love, marriage, and the family more than you want God himself, you probably need to re-examine who created perfect love, devoted lovers, and loving families. According to the book of Genesis, God gave Eve to Adam because God said in Genesis 2:18—And the LORD God said, "It is not good that the man should be alone; I will make him an help meet for him." KJV-Adam and Eve began family life together. Corruption occurred during the encounter with the serpent, the Tree of Knowledge, the forbidden fruit, and Adam and Eve's complicity. Such an encounter resulted in human bondage in effect, marital strife, familial conflict, and distressed relationships. In the aftermath of that encounter in the Garden of Eden, centuries later, we witness unending violence, broken lives, dysfunctional families, impoverished conditions, oppression, injustice and the list goes on describing how we treat one another in the human family. Some members of the human family earnestly believe that committed love between two people, genuine faithfulness in marriage, and harmony in the family can happen, and it can happen for human life in real time. Though it sometimes seems far out of reach for my own personal life, I still believe in love, marriage and the family—living, loving and giving of ourselves to improve the quality of human life. Nonetheless, I learned a profound truth about love and that truth I now commit to writing. I discovered and experienced the perfect love of God in my four decades of living a celibate lifestyle. I found greater peace and joy in each new day living according to the scriptures. God's perfect love delivered me from bitterness, unforgiveness, hostility, and internal agony.

You will read in this book accounts of how, in the past four decades, I curled up into the powerful strong arms of God and rested my soul. I studied the scriptures and surrendered to God's authority and power to transform my life. I listened to hundreds of sermons from different regions of the world. I learned to worship God uninhibitedly. I cried out to God for inner peace. I desperately wanted a God given extreme makeover. I did not like the woman that I had been in the past. My unrelenting desire to draw closer to God through the strategic, personal, academic, and small group study of scripture matured me both spiritually and emotionally. Finally, I accepted God's perfect love. Such love evidenced extravagantly to me, firmly establishing my commitment to total surrender. I wanted all of God. I relied upon God's guidance in daily life as the Holy Spirit taught me to explore healthy emotional relationships, virtuous choices, and wise decisions.

Of course, in my imperfection, I struggled with idiosyncratic issues in my personality. I gave all of them to God, and God is guiding me through such distracting insecurity issues in human relations as God grows my confidence in God's perfect love. What a journey filled with side-bar words of wisdom from strangers; stop-offs at public marketplace stations where I lingered reflecting upon lessons learned from previous relationships. Rushing to experience romantic love, marriage, and the family took me to a place of inquiry. Why did God allow some folks to experience love, marriage and the family and not others—that is others who deeply longed for this experience. God did not answer this question directly. I sensed that I did not need to know God's reasons for what happened to others. I had a father:daughter relationship with God through his son Jesus and I needed to concentrate on that. God's plan for my life is what I should completely embrace. In doing so, I will find my purpose for breathing in and out daily. God chose to show me what I would miss in the absence of first receiving his perfect love. I now sense the joy of perfect love way down deep in my soul that gives me peace—lasting, daily, unflappable peace. I learned the inner peace lesson after following a winding, weaving, and wearisome road that delivered me to the end of myself and the beginning of finding perfect love in God alone.

A Few More Details

In this book, you will read an account of how satisfaction intensifies in the humdrum of daily life. I actually move through my days excited to see how God's love will guide my decision-making in not only planning activities, but also in executing them. Because I turned to our Creator, Redeemer and Sustainer of life to meet my expectations, I turn away from such high expectations of my fellow humans. Alas, I interact more confidently with family, friends, colleagues, neighbors, and strangers. God's perfect love tempers my yearning for human love and companionship. Oh yes, the desire for love and marriage remains, but I now trust God with it!

As you continue to read my story, you will find that as an ordained minister of the gospel of Jesus Christ, I share with single women and even married women who long for the deeply satisfying love life from a soul mate and not finding it, I stand as a witness that one can find it in our God's perfect love. I found it in countries in Europe, Southeast Asia, the South Pacific Islands, Canada, Russia, Australia, Mexico, Brazil, Israel, Jordan and throughout the 47 states I visited in America.

Much of my musical taste and influence came from the rhythm and blues I listened to for countless hours. I cleaned my parent's house from the rafters to the underbelly crooning to those love ballads from America's greatest artists. I sang all kinds of music anticipating the day of my marriage, the birth of my babies and the life of our family. I sang gospel music, jazz, pop, country and western, show tunes as long as they talked about love. The more I sang the love songs, the cleaner our house would get. I found motivation, energy, and strength in the love songs and in my overactive imagination. I saw myself in the gym able to bench press 300 lbs. Because of the energy I gained at the very idea of family life. I felt energized singing about loving, caring, sharing, staying, belonging, communicating and being the one and only in my husband's life. Oh wow, my thoughts played tricks on this teenage romanticist. Those love songs sustained me as I thoroughly mopped, dusted, rearranged, scraped, organized and set our modest wooden home in good order.

Though the music probably wore on my mom's nerves, she patiently awaited the results of those overplayed ballads and exhaled at the beauty of her daughter's presentation of a pristinely cleaned house from top to bottom. I loved cleaning as a young girl. Perhaps it became symbolic of the need to cleanse my aching soul because I cluttered my emotions with ideas about love and marriage.

At the risk of exhausting you with any more of this introduction, needless to say, more than anything I pray you will find accounts of God's extravagant evidence in my life through his perfect love. You certainly have found evidence of my obsession with love. How good to know that I have overcome. I placed all of the aforementioned in the hands of a great and majestic God. I found security by doing so.

My story chronicles episodes in which poor judgment calls landed me in undesirable and sometimes menacing settings, potentially altering my holistic health. God's grace and mercy prevented many an emotional collapse. Several of my relationships with aspiring artists, who, like me, took wildly foolish risks frightened me. Nonetheless, I floundered into dark places of "cool" social gatherings where generous activities with free-spirited, wild-living friends extended throughout the night. Over a short period, night clubbing until 3:00 a.m., watching friends snort cocaine, looking at drunken men slobbering all over ingenues took its toll on every fiber of my character. I sensed the weight of life similar to the heaviness of those dental X Ray bibs. In the past, when the x-ray bib draped across my upper torso before an X Ray of my mouth, I sensed my weary shoulders speaking to me in those dental chairs as the X Ray bib draped across them pressing against my broken heart.

Who was this woman that I was becoming? Unrecognizable! In answering that question, my Christian roots spoke to my inner self. Compelled to find peace again with God and my soul, I sat down in my living room and pondered these two questions: "Why are you doing what you do these days? What do you really expect to gain?" In answering these questions, I bowed my head, bent my knees, and stretched my arms out in desperation before the God who had not allowed me to be utterly destroyed by the doors I opened that filled my soul with deep remorse. I simply lost my way. Naively, I followed a calamitous path, meandering through narrow alleys of ambition; flitting about through unmanageable venues. Fear gripped me. Faith grabbed me. God's love lingered in my heart even in my profound unworthiness.

By God's grace, I am alive and mentally sound. God's mercy prevented several emotional slam dunks from becoming my tragic end. Over many decades now, as with plants, I asked God to clip my dead leaves, prune my wilted or dead branches, purify my corrupted soil, and cause me to take deep roots and blossom into a garden of love, hope, joy, peace, and tenderheartedness. The journey began and Potter God picked up the pieces of this broken vessel and revived my soul again.

Thank you for both reading and sharing this book.

Sunny San Antonio

I will bless the Lord at all times; his praise shall continually be in my mouth. My soul makes her boast in the Lord; the humble shall hear thereof and be glad.
Psalm 34:1-2—King James Version

Early Years

Coming of age in the sunny, safe city of San Antonio in the grand expanse of flat land Texas birthed within me an unquenchable desire for family life. I knew at five years old that I wanted to marry and have a house full of children. Perhaps this desire, intensified by the fact that our house was always full of children, took root over the years in watching family shows. I love the variety of comedy shows that focus on family life. I confess, seeing women in pearls and heels at the kitchen sink quite fascinated me. My mom did not look like that as she was preparing our dinner. She wore a house dress instead.

Nonetheless, except for the fact that in my adolescent years, I did not see any black families with children on television, I thoroughly appreciated the multiple shows with the strong father figures, the fashionable moms and the delightful children with all of their antics. Mom did not permit more than an hour, occasionally two hours of television watching on any given evening. Following dinner with chores done as well as homework, we were able to see our favorite show. We all sat together in the living room. We all laughed together and good naturedly mimicked the behavior in the shows. Mom was always reading the paper. Dad was usually looking at his Sunday school books in preparation for his teaching tasks.

My own blended family consisted of my dad, whom we affectionately called Daddy. Daddy was a widower who had three independent adult children before he married our mom. Mom, whom we affectionately called Mother, experienced the widow's life early because her husband passed away before she reached her 30th birthday. Mom's first born son remained in Dallas, Texas with her parents for several years after mom relocated to San Antonio from Dallas, Texas. Mom and dad blended their families and soon found themselves rearing four more children together—Harold James [first oldest], CarolAnn [second oldest], Edwin Kenneth [my baby brother], and Deborah Lynn [my baby sister]. Our household, filled with music, kept us singing with our mom at the piano, or playing and singing to records, and finally listening to the radio all throughout our years at home together. Harold and I studied piano for a few years. Harold's skills surpassed mine and he set the tone for achieving excellence in every adventure of our lives.

I found joy in the adult children of my Daddy as well as my bonus sister's own children, some older than I. My Daddy, twenty-four years older than my mom, parented a daughter, Estelle, and two sons, Damon and Hoover. We did not get to know Damon but we did enjoy wonderful visits from Hoover and his wife and sometimes later, their two children. My eldest bonus sister, Estelle Campbell married John Campbell in her young years. They parented ten children—Mary, Eugene, Thomas, Johnnie Mae, Larry, Beverly, Jeannetta, Esther, John Jr., and Estella. Because the Campbells lived about an hour away in my Daddy's hometown of Luling, Texas, we did not get to see them often. We longed to spend more time with them. When they visited with us, they brought laughter, fun and antics. When we visited with them, we loved their hometown, but found city life more to our liking. Though Luling was lush with vegetation, we missed all of the neighborhoods which surrounded our sunny street with flower gardens and children on sidewalks roller skating and riding bicycles.

Though Harold was an only child for a while living with my mom's parents, he enjoyed his father's family. He had a grandmother, Susie Clark, and two aunts—Lillie and Lizzie. They treasured their relationship with Harold and saw so much of their beloved Ike, Harold's dad, in Harold's personality. We enjoyed being invited to visit Grandmother Clark, Aunt Lillie and Aunt Lizzie in Dallas, my mom's hometown. The journey from San Antonio to Dallas on the train thrilled me. The long passenger cars and wide windows and our deep cushioned seats with feet kicking room kept me bouncing about as the train rolled down the tracks with plenty of Texas flat lands, blue bonnets, cattle farms and barns to study all along the way.

I remember Grandmother Clark's home on the corner of Latimer Street in big Dallas. Such warm, comfortable, spacious rooms with high ceilings and lovely window dressings—like in the movies—their comfy, colorful corner home amazed me. As an aspect of southern charm, their wrap-around porch attracted my attention and occupied my time. I imagined myself with a large family in a home just like that one. I loved Grandmother Clark, Aunt Lillie and Aunt Lizzie. They cooked plenty of the most scrumptious food and desserts that I usually did not get to eat. My mom remained quite fanatical about food intake—high blood pressure, diabetes, hypertension and other health related matters she believed both began and intensified with food intake. We ate luxuriously in Dallas. Then we returned home to our simpler diets and simply seasoned foods—a little salt and pepper and that's about it. We drank water most nights and counted it a delicacy to have Kool-Aid from time to time. I did not know that we were "poor." I did know that doctors, lawyers, teachers, Sleeping Car Porters, government employees and entrepreneurs had bigger, better houses than we had.

We mixed our visits with the Clark family with adventures in my mom's parents' home at 4928 Tracy Street in the Booker T. community of Dallas. If I remember my experiences accurately, this Booker T community was across the tracks and down the hill, slightly in the valley, a short distance from Highland Park, the exclusive and wealthy community where the white folks lived. The contrast between the houses and surroundings in Highland Park and mom's Booker T community raised my consciousness regarding the racial divide. I received quite an education when I walked up the hill, across the tracks, around the corners and onto the sidewalks of the Highland Park area.

I feared that sometimes the homeowners did not want me to walk on their sidewalks. In this way, they sometimes stood in their doorway with a simpler outer door between my scrawny body and their 80 pound pedigree dog appearing just moments from the command to fly out the door onto my skinny adolescent bare legs. I squeezed my hands tightly and walked right down the sidewalks trusting angels to watch over me. Afterall, we sang that song in church, about angels watching over us day and night. I wanted to gaze upon those houses and dream about owning one, so I braved the possibility of being frightened by those big dogs seemingly staring down at me from every other window or door. The houses appeared to be large enough to accommodate my imaginary family of some eight children and just maybe I would have big dogs too.

Nevertheless, in the Booker T community, I faced the reality of our then lifestyles. I appreciated that my siblings, cousins, aunts, uncles, grandparents and I enjoyed plenty of love, laughter and even good labor in our grandparents' home. The story telling peaked our curiosity about our mom's siblings and their childhood there at the homefront. We often supported my Granny with the hard work that she faced. One thing that bothered me about my Granny's work was the huge tub of clothes from the white folks that Granny washed in the backyard over a woodfire. I did not like getting that close to a blazing fire; and, I definitely resented having to stir the clothes around and about in the soapy water. That part of our labor I wanted to forget. I wished that my Granny did not have to work like that for more than six decades of her life. Over the years, my grandmother's hands showed the riveting effects of hand washing the clothes of the white folks that lived in the Highland Park community.

What a learning curve for me when I helped Granny with those heavy cotton clothes. I especially resented my tasks because I loved my long beautiful finger nails. I prized how they made my hands look and I did not want to disturb their beauty. How laughable when I think of such things today. I prized my fingernails over what that manual labor did to my Granny's hands, back, knees, brow, hair and her feet too. Sizzling sun, boiling water over a wooden fire, rocky earth soil beneath her feet, perspiration dripping into her towel and apron to prevent the sweat from falling into the tub of clothes. My Granny took the best care of those rich white folks' clothes and all I wanted to do was protect my fingernails. Selfishness reigns. Sigh.

While my maternal Granny worked as "The Help" for several prominent families in wealthy neighborhoods in Dallas, our Papa, the Rev. Jack Corney, pastored a church in Dallas, and participated in civic matters on behalf of the Booker T community. Rev. Jack Corney earned respect in his community and the church because he both pastored and planted African Methodist Episcopal churches in Dallas and surrounding areas. He thrived on guiding churches to fuller development and greater participation in the community. He enjoyed advocating for public works and related services in the Booker T community. He did not fear the wrath of the white elected officials and administrators. He believed that he could appeal to reason. He endured insults in order to get the appropriate attention and correction to the needs of his community.

Mom told us that on one occasion, the Booker T community needed critical attention to the sewage systems in their blocks. Families were no longer using outhouses. Their indoor toilets and plumbing systems needed appropriate sewage pipelines and the department of public works had ignored the pleas of individual households. Neighbors summoned Rev. Corney and encouraged him to go to meet with the staff of public works. My grandfather, affectionately called Papa, went to the Public Works office and—though he sat and waited for several hours—found himself ignored by the staff. On the third day of his visit, where he sat in the office all day as he had done on the previous two days, he not only read his books, but also he smoked his pipe. After a short while, he used the spittom in the corner of the front office. Interestingly enough, Papa saw the top manager within an hour after his spittom incident. The problems in the Booker T. community with the sewage system, corrected soon after the meeting, put Papa in even greater demand for problem solving in the Booker T. community. My mom got the biggest laugh out of telling us that story. How amazing to know that happened free of any physical altercation or profound verbal abuse in the early 1900's to a black preacher in Texas in his black suit, white shirt and black tie, tophat and a pipe smoker. I noticed Papa's library in the modest Corney residence. Papa surrounded himself with books and became a self-taught leader. I wondered if his library inspired my mom, who was quite an avid reader.

On the other hand, our Granny did not spend much time reading. Instead, she washed, starched and ironed her husband's white shirts. She traveled back and forth to the market to purchase fresh meat, fruits, and vegetables. She stood over the stove and prepared meals to perfection. She baked pies and cookies. She cared for her children and her neighbors as she became aware of their needs. She nurtured her children and modeled Christian character before them. As a dutiful wife, doting mother and loving grandmother, we respected Granny as well as feared her response if we, her grandchildren, disobeyed. She did not take kindly to rebellious behavior in her grandchildren. Her 4'8" frame seemed to expand significantly when she disciplined us.

While some of the men in our family, including my Daddy, shared meal and kitchen tasks, Papa did not. Papa, the intellectual, needed space to sit and think as he prepared sermons, administered church business, conducted civic duties and ensured that his family had all of their needs met. Granny seemed more than satisfied to care for her home, cook, clean, wash, iron, garden, and share with her grandchildren. My mom shared stories about the fifty years her parents sustained their marriage before Papa's death in 1955. My mom cherished, admired and supported emotionally her six siblings— Edwin, Helen, William, Dorothy, Richard and Esther. Nothing seemed more wonderful than family time with both my mom and Daddy's families in two different areas of Texas. Dallas, big and bustling with energy and activity; Luling, quiet, simple and refreshing with plenty of space to run and watch the animal and farm life— both affirming the young woman that I was becoming.

After my initial experience in New York at the tender age of 16, I spent years with "my other mother" my Mom's baby sister, Esther Brown and her family—Uncle Gene, Ronnie and Kathi in

New York City. I traveled alone by Greyhound bus from San Antonio to New York City as a brand new sixteen year old, over protected, trusting southern girl. Most of my journey remained incident free. Unfortunately one bus driver, during a change of buses in Ohio did misinform me about the destination of his bus. A white male passenger on that bus overheard the driver misinform me about the destination of his bus. That kind gentleman looked graciously upon me—a wide-eyed, smiling, innocent, unsuspecting southern girl making her way. Graciously, the passenger advised me that I needed to go to the next lane and that the bus there would take me directly to New York City. I discovered that day that God provided angels for his sons and daughters. That white male passenger became an angel to this curious and intimidated solo traveler en route to the big city. That gentleman saved me many hours of extra riding. Afterall, the ride from San Antonio to New York was already 48 hours. In my eagerness to arrive both safely and soon, I needed to be sure that the destination panel on the bus was the one that would get me directly to New York City. God provided that angel in Ohio when I had to change buses. I finally arrived at New York's Port Authority—wide-eyed, jaw dropped and immediately captivated by the energy in the city—I concluded that, in the future, I would live in New York. And I did.

At sixteen, my adventures in the Polo Grounds and Rangel Houses at 159-64 Harlem River Drive with Aunt Esther and the extended Brown family changed the trajectory of my life. My brief encounter with Ronnie and Kathi who were on their way to Florida to spend their summer with their dad's family members left me hopeful to get to know them better. In their absence, Aunt Esther and Uncle Gene acquainted me with their children through plenty of stories and pictures. I thought that Aunt Esther and Uncle Gene were rich because they never mentioned that they did not have enough money to do all of the things that summer that we did in New York. I cherished every minute of my time with them. I saw so much of New York on my own because both my aunt and uncle were working. Aunt Esther left directions for me every day to take the subway to a tourist attraction in Manhattan. I did not venture on my own to any other borough. Riding the subway felt quite exotic as I encountered the diversity and multiple curious personalities quite different to those I had known thus far during my youth in San Antonio. Listening to gifted musicians in the subway station and on sidewalks fascinated me. Inhaling roasted peanuts, pretzels, onions, pizzas, hot dogs, as I walked past dozens of food vendors and sidewalk merchants enhanced my appetite to eat more than I had ever eaten in life.

On another note, my Aunt Esther sustained her commitment to the AME church tradition of our family. As a member of the church, among other ministries, Aunt Esther joined the choir, became a class leader and organized bus outings to Lake George and Saratoga Springs for summer getaways. She treasured music. In this way, I met some of the most gifted tenors, sopranos, altos, and baritones in New York at both Mother AME Zion, Aunt Esther's family church, and Abyssinian Baptist Churches, the church I joined when I lived in New York. I always chased rainbows, my friends said. I always sought out the highly visible and more popular places and leaders. I suspect that I did so. My aunt took me to hear the most magnificent choirs at Salem United Methodist and Convent Avenue Baptist church. I embraced my experiences at The Greater Refuge Temple with my Aunt Peggy. Attending church services, concerts and related activities left quite a fingerprint on my spiritual interests during my summer of 1963 in New York. Aunt Esther's daughter Kathi and her son Ronnie actively participated in every aspect of the church's life. Because of the meaningful experiences as a teenager at Mother AME Zion, I felt compelled to give more serious thought to my spiritual formation. The groundwork, laid by my Daddy and mom, and early church related experiences provided a sure foundation for pursuing a Christ following lifestyle. Jesus Christ, I knew deep within that no escape awaited me from making Christ my Savior.

More Back Story

I need to share a little more about my childhood in San Antonio. As a young girl, I learned to love music. Our home, filled with my mom's piano playing and singing of her favorite hymns, my Daddy's prayers and scripture readings, my older brother's "doo wop" singing, my younger siblings singing in choirs at church and in citywide choirs, and my own experiences as both a church pianist and choir director filled my life with all kinds of music—from classical, sacred, gospel, jazz, blues, folk, bluegrass to Broadway show tunes. Somehow my mom and Daddy managed their money well enough for us to have all kinds of music to play on record players, the piano and hand instruments. We sang through adversity, hardship, disappointments, Christmas celebrations, Easter services and productions, summer recreation, and all other family and community joyful occasions. I did not know that we were categorized as a working class family until I became a senior in high school. With the kind of music that filled our heart and home, we seemed to be quite rich to me. We awakened to music, sang in the car rides, sang at school, sang in playtime. So much singing seemed to punctuate everything that we did throughout the day.

Daddy and mom showed us how to share with family members in spite of what seemed to be limited resources for us. Mom bought enough groceries to share specific items with her sister Dorothy. Though Aunt Dorothy worked at Kelly Field Air Force Base, mom wanted to ensure that as a single parent, she lacked no essentials. Aunt Dorothy and her daughters, Beverly and Pam, brought great joy to our lives then and now. They had lived in Brooklyn in their toddler years and relocated to San Antonio before their primary grades. When we first met them, we really carried on with them as we listened curiously to their New York accents. I found them to be rather exotic because I only heard the southern dialect except for Sister Rosetta who had a pronounced Irish accent.

Any discussion of my childhood without pointing to our terrific neighbors would be a disservice to my childhood and teen years. In this way, I respected the Nolan, Dawson, Blue Bonnet, Burnett, and Hays Street neighbors in San Antonio. These families conjoined with our family circle and extended our community lifestyles. We roamed about the community from porch to porch or street to street checking in on friends and finding recreational activities to share. Seldom did we go to one another's houses—no need to do so because

San Antonio weather invited you to spread your wings in the out-doors—skating, playing jacks on concrete steps, reading comics on porches, playing cards on card tables, engaging with arts and crafts on porches and the like. I focused upon Nolan and Dawson Street neighbors because I knew them longer and more intimately—the Gonzales, the Dibrells, the Jacksons, the Harrises, the Browns, the Thompsons, Ms. Eddie Mae and her husband, the Smiths, the Westons, Mr. McNeil and in my teen years, the Michael family. The Michael family [their paternal grandmother. "Big Mama," Aunt Cris, Sharon, Elzie Jr., Baby Brother, James Otis, and Sadie Joann] joined our neighborhood during my high school years. They brought fun, fellowship and plenty of adventure. We share a loving extended fam-ily friendship nearly six decades later. What a joy to watch their pro-ductive and fulfilling lives unfold.

These precious and loving families shared life with us during our informative years in the 1700 block of Nolan Street. The hus-bands and wives of the aforementioned names spoke firmly to us. They reinforced the values that they knew our parents taught us. No foolishness found acceptance among these forthright neighbors who fiercely verbally disciplined us if they saw us behaving destructively. From our neighbors perspective, my siblings and I committed the worst crimes by walking on the neighbors manicured lawns or play-ing ball in the street or plucking flowers from their flower gardens. Those things caused us tongue lashings. That was about the extent of our misbehavior. In the 50's and 60's, we had much bible study and prayer in our lives. In this way, we always felt God's eyes upon us. Our neighbors reinforced every ideal, virtue, value and sentiment that they embraced which mirrored our parents' teachings. They shared in shaping us into productive, law-abiding, morally sound, Christ oriented citizens with selfless attitudes to serve and meet the needs of others. Our neighbors modeled this behavior in such gra-cious ways. We shared fruits, vegetables, meats, nuts [pecans from the trees], desserts, baked goods, sometimes clothes and household items as needed.

The Gonzales family affectionately known as Mr. and Mrs. G and their son, Doug, bridged the gap for our youngest brother's recreational and adventure needs. Their only son became our bonus brother. Accordingly, my brother, Edwin K., was always invited to join Mr. G and Doug on excursions experiencing hunting, fishing, hiking, and "boy sports" events. When the entire G family visited museums and other cultural events, Edwin K joined them as Doug's travel companion. Doug was always the tallest kid in the group and Edwin K was scrawny and shorter. These two guys were such fun to watch, especially at basketball. Edwin K, a great competitor, never let anything prevent him from working diligently to compete. He loved to share with Doug and the bigger boys and he held his own.

In Doug's teen years, Mr. G purchased a standard pool table and, on his beautifully paved driveway in the backyard, we learned to shoot pool. That pool table got more than its share of wear and tear from the North siblings. Good-natured Doug shared his extra special toys and endured all of our laughter and banter as we generously played with them. Mr. and Mrs. G, until their deaths remained in our mind the kindest, most supportive and loving neighbors to our family. Surely the G family was the answer to my Daddy's prayers for they were angels on loan to us. They bridged gaps in major aspects of our lives where our financial situation simply could not do what the G family did for us. They provided unrelenting support—in emergencies, transportation failures, grocery shortages and other unexpected matters. They behaved toward us as their cherished family members and we wholeheartedly appreciated them.

The Levi and Rae Adel Jackson family poured their lives passionately into the entire North family. The Jackson family consisted of 7 sisters, one brother and two wonderfully warm and welcoming parents. On one occasion, my mom's oldest sister Helen brought her five boys to visit with us. What joy to see the five Murray brothers interact with the five oldest Jackson sisters. What a fun-filled visit for us. As an incurable romanticist, I began to envision courting possibilities between some of the Murray brothers and the Jackson sisters. Over the years, life went different ways for all of them. They married others. I lingered with the idea for a time and wondered what might have been.

Nonetheless, we had plenty of fun together during the brief encounters of these two families. The Jacksons otherwise became bonus sisters and a brother and the friendship continues more than six decades later. My mom found total fulfillment in her relationship with both Mr. Levi and Mrs. Rae Adel. Interestingly enough, Mr. Levi talked about international affairs and politics with my mom. Mrs. Rae Adel talked about the bible and scripture revelation with my Daddy. Mom and Mrs. Rae Adel must have talked about everything else in the world because they talked and talked forever until Mrs. Rae Adel passed unexpectedly in her early 50's.

My mom grieved her loss for many, many years. She loved all of her friends whom she kept from her young adult life until their deaths. There were many. If you gave me a piece of 8x10 notebook paper right this minute, I could write on that paper the names of many of my mom's friends, recalling their geographical locations, their occupations and their family members too. None of her friends—near and far—seemed to touch mom's heart in the way that Mrs. Rae Adel did. They both must have taken all of their secrets to their graves. My mom lived nearly fifty years longer than Mrs. Rae Adel. She took great solace in continuing her relationships with her beloved friends' children. We shared mom's vision for these lifetime friendships and we certainly remain connected to the Jackson daughters. The son passed away much sooner than we expected. He provided wisdom and leadership to his sisters and extended family throughout his lifetime. We took great pride in learning that he received his Ph.D. from the University of Texas in his latter years. He inspired all of us to pursue our dreams over our lifetime and not be bound by age.

As children, we never knew what all those long over the fence, over the telephone, at the dining room table talks between my mom and her friend meant. Perhaps they solved world problems and exchanged wisdom with one another regarding their daily journeys. Perhaps they talked through their personal issues with one another and arrived at places of safety and rest for the demands on their schedules and their lives. Whatever it was, they surely found comfort in their sisterhood. Remembering their relationship compels me to mimic that same commitment to my sister's friends across the nation and the world. Sisterhood soothes and refreshes. I have found it so.

Learning to love each other and each other's families along the way, watching our mom navigate her many friendships in the community and the church, left quite an impression on the North siblings. We discovered in our early lives that loving each other's families brought great benefits and hundreds of hours of joy. My mom's commitment to sustain her friendships until they passed away inspired all four of her children to do the same. My siblings and I enjoy the Jackson girls, now women, remembering their deceased sister Evelyn, and their brother, Levi Julius Jr. now that we are the senior citizens in one another's lives.

The Church placed front and center in our family culture. Our experiences in the church reflected a second aspect of our character development. After family life, the church occupied a place of significant spiritual development. We experienced two different church denominations in our home. Our mom, the preacher's kid, played the piano during her youth and young adult life at her father's churches in Dallas. Faithful to the AME church, we attended East St. Paul Methodist church around the corner from our home. Following a tragic automobile accident that left our Daddy at 57 years old, a carpenter by trade, now with an amputated right hand, East St. Paul reached out to our family to bridge the financial gap left with my dad's new normal. The gracious support they provided to our family eased tensions. Our dad adjusted to his prosthesis [he was right-handed] and the demands for a different kind of work. My siblings and I do not recall a time when Daddy mentioned his accident or the prosthesis. He went about his newly found work as a porter in a private lodge where members met to socialize and conduct civic affairs.

Daddy performed his duties as if he were cleaning the church for Jesus' arrival. My brothers, who sometimes cleaned the facilities with our Daddy, quarreled with him about his minute details and the commitment to thoroughly clean that lodge. They explained to him that the members did not appreciate anything that he did. They went on to tell him that the members probably didn't even notice how meticulously Daddy cleaned, buffed, polished, scraped, dusted and scrubbed that lodge every single day. My Daddy simply explained to his sons that he was cleaning that lodge as unto the Lord. He offered his best work to that group of men and ensured that their meeting place was more than clean for them. Though my brothers still took issue with Daddy's work ethic, they discovered that it became their own work ethic during their respective careers. All four of my mom and Daddy's children excelled in their careers. My brothers in corporate America; my baby sister, the social worker, and I, the educator/missionary gave our best efforts to those who needed our help. We all worked passionately to make a difference in the lives of others.

I learned Christian character from the many different teachers and pastors at East St. Paul. I especially remember the pastoral leadership of Rev. James Minor and his wife Sister Helen Minor. They parented five children—Miriam, Anderson, David, James and Timothy. That family captivated my attention. They reminded me of the television families that touched my heart. I loved how Sister Minor, who like some of the television mothers, spoke lovingly and wisely to her children. I respected how Pastor Minor, like some of the television sitcom fathers, nurtured his sons and daughter right before the eyes of those who kept watching his children come of age. Observing this godly couple, who provided stellar leadership to our church family, strengthened my own resolve to become a wife and mother as soon as I grew up. Family life occupied hours of my imagination. I often wondered why this issue captured so much of my mental energy.

My family and I appreciated the loving friendships formed at East Saint Paul Methodist Church: the Sheffields, the Hendersons, the Hines, the Browns, the Jacksons, the Turks, the Moores, the Davises, the Whites, the Williams, and over the years the many pastors and their families. Now that I am a senior citizen, I often reflect on those childhood days and the cherished memories of the many precious families that I loved and from whom I learned how to become a witness and follower of Christ. With church life as an attractive aspect of my spiritual development, I loved to play the hymns, the traditional gospel songs, and even some of the classical pieces that my brother, Harold, played. During my early teen years,

Sister Ella Lee Harris and Pastor Joe Nathan Harris took an interest in my piano skills. Sister Harris asked me to come and play for the services at Joshua Baptist Church during their interim search for a full time musician.

Both at Joshua and later at Second Baptist Church, I played piano and directed choirs. Pastor Joe Nathan Harris provided wise counsel at Joshua Baptist Church. Pastor Samuel H. James provided insightful preaching and teaching at Second Baptist Church. I also loved my time with my Daddy at his church: Healing Temple Church of God in Christ, under the leadership of Elder Duhart and in later years, with Elder Ward. I learned about the scriptures, the Judeo-Christian ethics, biblical principles, church hymnology, prayer, the Holy Ghost, speaking in tongues, praise, love, unity and God's will while attending all of my churches. I loved serving as the pianist for a season at Joshua Baptist Church thanks to the gorgeous love and example of Sister Ella Lee Harris, and at Second Baptist Church thanks to the gracious, kind and supportive teaching of Mrs. Ruth Burns. I served as a pianist for a respectable time in the aforementioned churches. Had I applied more time, attention, practice and study to my piano lessons, taught by Mrs. Hughie Dorn, and organ lessons, taught by Brother Smith, I suspect I may never have been without a job as a church musician.

Before the shock of having to be withdrawn due to financial concerns, I and my younger brother attended St. Peter Claver Academy. My youngest brother and I enjoyed our days as Catholic school attendees. As a first grader, I thought of Sister Rosetta as an angel in a nun's habit. She always spoke to this little eager eyed, happy faced, brown girl with a joyful lyric sound in her Irish brogue—"CarolAnn, you're so smart." The more she told me that, the harder I worked in my classroom to become her best student. By contrast, in the 3rd grade, Reverend Mother did not tell me that, but she did strike my knuckles with "Sister Blue" the round blue peg from a broken chair painted sky blue and used to strike the knuckles of students who turned in sloppy work or who misbehaved in any way. At least I learned from Reverend Mother NEVER to submit sloppy papers with strikeovers and scratched our words. Sigh.

My parents modeled the abiding love of God evidenced in their community sharing. My mom baked, roasted and fried foods that she could share with her family and the neighbors: cookies, bread, vegetables, fruits, eggs, chickens, roast beef, chili, beans, fish, pies, cakes and more. Watching my Daddy use his prosthesis to spread the tomato plant and collard green seeds in his vegetable gardens intrigued me. My Daddy's prosthesis in the '50's, '60's and '70's remained a rarity. When our curious friends saw our dad at the front door, they often jumped back at the sight of his "Captain Hook" right arm. We forgot that our dad even had a missing right hand.

My mother thrived on taking care of people and plants. She, therefore, found herself planting flowers in her garden every chance she got. She loved potted plants and flower gardens and tended to them with such loving care as she watched them grow just like she watched her children getting taller and stronger. I followed mom's lead. In New York City, I had 32 house plants that provided a gorgeous sight as they framed the bay window in my apartment. I played music for my plants and talked to them. They grew beautifully and sensed my moods all the time. What a wonderful sense of achievement to watch our plants growing from 3 inches to 3 feet. All living creatures fascinate me.

We did not have the financial portfolios of my middle class friends. We did enjoy countless hours of joy with our music, singing, sports, church activities and family adventures. Our parents struggled to meet their budget, but I did not know that we were poor. We certainly had enough to eat, desirable clothes and could join in the fun with the multiple school and community related activities in which we were involved. I realized our financial limitations when I saw the kind car that my parents could afford—a used 2 door Ford beautifully painted sky blue. Mom named our car Betsy. Sometimes Betsy provided reliable transportation. Many times Betsy limped along with first one repair needed and then another. I watched my mom patiently work with unreliable Betsy until my mom transitioned from the position of a Nurse's Aide to that of a Registered Nurse. Mom amazed everyone when she returned to college at 44 and graduated at 48 becoming one of San Antonio's first black Registered Nurses. What an achievement in 1962.

I hope that each reader gets a glimpse of my early years and family life from this section of the book. My missteps did not begin during my childhood or teen years. I submitted to the authority of my parents. I did not rebel against their teachings. I followed the rules and honored their expectations. My upbringing landed me in good spaces and places during my high school and four year college matriculation. After my undergraduate studies, I soon found myself in a series of missteps—uncertain about my personal and professional direction. I found myself moving away from the excellent home training and effective parenting skills and following a path of "rain-bow chasing." In my mind, I should become a qualified professional in a career path, reaching goals in media or theater. Psychologically, I seemed to be struggling with my stifling insecurities.

Regrettably my missteps intensified after a few different per-sonal and social traumatic events during my early twenties. I lost myself in the process of working through some of my trauma. I lost touch with the core of my being. I began to question God, chal-lenge my own moral fiber, resent my Christian heritage and resist the teachings and expectations of my parents. The social/political issues in America, externally, and my spiritual warfare, internally, resulted in missteps that could easily have cost me my life. God's love and the extravagant evidence thereof transformed my life beginning with my full surrender to him.

The chapters going forward share both my transformation pro-cess and evidence of not just God's perfect love but God's extrava-gance toward one that hungered so desperately for love, marriage and the family.

Burdens: Blessings

Bless the LORD, O my soul, and forget not all his benefits:
who forgiveth all thine iniquities; who healeth all thy diseases;
who redeemeth thy life from destruction; who crowneth
thee with lovingkindness and tender mercies; who satisfieth
thy mouth with good things; so that thy youth is renewed
like the eagle's. Psalm 103:2-5—King James Version

The Back Story

In the late spring of 1977, I stood in the middle of my sunlit spacious living room floor in my apartment [Hotel Brewster] at 21 West 86th Street [between Central Park West and Columbus Avenue] in New York City. This address and the apartment on the 15th floor with a building directly in front of me that was only nine floors high illustrates the extravagant evidence of God's Love for me even after I abandoned God. The unblocked southern exposure allowed for soothing sunlight nourishing all of my 32 plants that lined my picture glass window with its wings on the left and right. Too, the panoramic view of Central Park and other surroundings thrilled my light sensitive soul. Of course, I could not afford this apartment. I worked two jobs to meet the miserable New York monthly rent for this gorgeous apartment with a living room/dining room 30' x 15'; a bedroom 15' x 18' and a bathroom 6' x9'. Wow. My fellow artists lived in apartments with rooms the size of my bathroom. God did it again, in spite of my backslidden state.

Whenever I struggled to meet my expenses, my beloved, patient, generous boyfriend, Bennie, bridged the gap. How, in retrospect, I wish that I had treated him much better than I did. I remember being such a nasty soul with him. I hate that I lashed out at him, bear mauling his emotions, and lacerating his kindnesses with my own miserable frustrations piled high from the rigors of pursuing both a recording and Broadway contract. How repentant I am that I did not seize the opportunity to treat him well while time permitted. Twists and turns in life took us apart and I never returned his love, though over the years, he did forgive me for my crummy behavior.

Life passes all too quickly and repeat performances do not often occur. What needs to happen in the moment, must happen so that we can find places of quiet rest for our souls. I never had the privilege of treating Bennie like a king. He deserved such treatment from me. Perhaps his forgiveness is all that I have left. It suffices in small measure. Recalling his patient, kind and gracious love toward me and my impatient, self-serving, abrasive, inconsistent feigned affection toward him spoiled my romantic life going forward. I paid a price for how poorly I treated this dear soul. I think of him often. Some behavior in life gets etched into the soul of a person. Going forward means that you take the scar tissue from times when your verbal and emotional wounds toward another critically wounded you as well. How I wish I did not know so much about what I am sharing with my readers. I know more than I can tell. I hope this helps someone.

Inasmuch as I believed that a talent agent and a potential recording or Broadway contract beckoned me, I concluded that I would not cook much. I, therefore, decided to eat plenty of fresh fruits, vegetables, nuts, grains and salads. Purchasing hot soups from the nearby Greek restaurant and baked goods from the nearby bakery suited my lifestyle. Besides, I continued to date my devoted Bennie, who preferred to spend money earned through his floor service, at restaurants of his clients and friends. I enjoyed being his dining companion with no disappointment in our cuisines.

I decorated my apartment with rich, warm colors of hunter green, deep copper or fiery tangerine, chocolate brown and stunning champagne. On the floor where I preferred to sit, I felt the comfort of the extra padded short shag carpet of a deep red-orange color that was a feast for my eyes. Along the perfectly rectangular shaped front corner of my apartment stood some 32 plants on the ledge of the spacious window sill. These plants, affectionately called my children, graced the tall front picture windows and trailed over to the right and left of the window sill on self-standing wrought iron, wooden, and colorful ceramic plant stands. The plants reflected my mood swings like mirrors reflecting facial agony. "My children" exposed my dark and gray emotional areas as they wilted or even turned from their natural colors. What a mystery to watch the plants behave in such exotic ways. On any given day after another cast call in an over-crowded room of "wanna be" fellow artists, I listened attentively for my name.

Returning home from more grueling auditions, I slumped dejected into my high back, cushioned incidental chair, reflecting upon how disappointed I felt that I heard every name except mine at another humiliating casting call. I actually hated those casting calls, but inevitably I faced them to see what hand I would be dealt in show business. Alas, after each one, I lifted my chin, smiled through anguish at the hopefuls, and dragged my aggravated soul back to my gorgeous apartment. There I grabbed my chocolate chip cookies, plopped on my living room floor, after popping my cassette of classi-cal music in the cassette player, and sang longingly to my plants. My plants blossomed, spread their leaves, stood tall, grew beautifully as they stretched out to the edges of my carpet and draped themselves across the parquet wooden floors. I beamed joyfully to have this much of nature smiling at me before I concluded that I might make a call back at the very next casting call. The challenge remained for non Actor's Equity Association members to prayerfully be the right fit for the nearly fully cast musical, drama or comedy. Most roles, I was told, were cast by directors who knew exactly the persons they wanted for the show. Agents then had the upper hand for the remaining cast-ing needs. Occasionally, a "wanna be" like me caught an incredi-bly "lucky" break and found him or herself cast as an unknown in quite a prominent role. So I hoped for that kind of day at the next OPEN casting call for either a Broadway or Off Broadway show. I remember thinking so often: what a long, lonely, lingering labyrinth to stardom. I asked myself these questions: "Is it really worth it? How badly do you want this?" I knew just working in some small off, off Broadway show or some traveling band, or some small theater workshop would never satisfy my desire for STARDOM. I determined that only a Broadway, Tony award winning performance, Grammy nomination/win, Oscar nomination/win, applause, applause, stellar review career or NOTHING marked the destiny for this kiddo. That kind of thinking probably blocked my blessings. Maybe!

Actually, I confess that once again God's love showed me extravagant evidence. Though I graduated from Fisk University with a Bachelor of Arts degree in 1969; matriculated one semester at the University of Pittsburgh in the Master's degree program in the School of Communications; and completed some thirty hours of coursework in the Student Personnel Administration in Higher Education Master's program at Howard University, I chose to abandon reason and make my way to New York City to pursue a career on Broadway. My ego prompted me to follow my Broadway dreams after my DC Black Repertory Theater days. Too, during the summer of 1973, at Arena Stage, my role in Raisin, the musical, as the Understudy to Virginia Capers, Mama, and to Mrs. Johnson, the neighbor, boosted my confidence in my vocal talents. In retrospect, I got ahead of myself. I should have remained with the DC Black Repertory Theater company for at least two more years. Perhaps my theatrical preparation and vocal confidence needed more off Broadway tweaking.

Nonetheless, I abandoned the opportunities to become gainfully employed according to my educational background. I concluded that a professional position would hinder my flexibility to be available for casting calls. In this way, I recognized the need to sign on with temporary help agencies. In the 70's in NYC, temporary office help provided large corporations and businesses with highly skilled employees. Such persons afforded the companies to reduce their budget because temps, as we became known, did not qualify for benefits. Too, temps could be expeditiously terminated avoiding costly legal proceedings. I knew this; but, I reassured myself that I would become "a STAR" as a temp because of my work ethic, integrity, and personality. I landed the most fulfilling daily temp assignments and earned the kind of money that met my budgetary needs.

Those temp assignments represent some of the most wonderful work days of my life. As a temp, I miss the lighthearted fun on the job. As a temp, I avoided office politics. As a temp, I arrived refreshed every morning in each new setting. As a temp, I could treat everyone like MVP's because I might not get to see them again. Temp life added richness to my career. It took the sting out of the rejections from theater life. Once again extravagant evidence of God's love filled the cracks in my career path.

Since earning enough money to meet New York rent remained the burgeoning cry of many of us in the theater, I searched for money earning avenues that supported my sense of decency. Invited by a neighbor to make brown paper bag drops in flights to and from Central America did not make the list. Cajoled to be the weekly sexual exploit of a male who had money but no time for details, just sexual exploits, pay and go heightened my horror at just how broken one can become. I said NO thank you to that possibility too. Unending invitations by my Jewish landlord to be a playmate for some of his business partners sickened me way down deep in my soul. I turned gently away from that discussion at the desk of my landlord as I appealed for just one more week of grace for my past due rent. Laughingly, but all too seriously, one fellow artist suggested that I take advantage of the BIG money offered to women who would pose nude for sordid men's magazines. I shunned, bucked and vomited at the thought of that adventure. I left God but I remembered my Daddy's prayers: "I will keep you on the altar until God's spirit shakes you up and causes you to rush back into his arms."

Seeking avenues to earn more money resulted in a tempting offer from a friend. She happened to be a fellow Texan who had relocated to NYC to break into theater. She advised me of a perfect job for earning enough money to pay rent and have enough financial freedom to do something special for yourself. She told me the address of a bar in the lower Manhattan area where she made substantial tips as a cocktail waitress. She said her earning power rivaled that of some business executives. Since I resisted the opportunity to be reconciled to my boyfriend, I thought I might meet someone new and earn money among this evening business men crowd who let their hair down after work at this bar in their neighborhood. I asked a male buddy of mine to take me to this bar to both meet up with my friend and to survey the situation.

Wow, when I arrived, I sensed danger. Not the kind of danger brought by violence, drug use, gunfire or of that nature, but the kind of violence that spoke to my soul in these words: "You, CarolAnn, may now be reaching the point of no return if you become invested in earning money in this place. I felt immediately harrassed by the heat of salacious acts and unbridled sexual contacts. Like a tsunami, the behavior of the scantily clothed dancer on the small stage in close proximity to the male audience suggested nothing was off limits. Like a matador against the bull, she hurled her black fabric sex cover through the sexually charged, alcohol enhanced atmosphere. Suddenly a man built like a defensive linebacker rushed to the stage and fell to his knees where the dancer then squatted like a toddler at the potty. She draped the black cloth across the upper torso of this muscle bound man. Before his head was covered he profusely salivated and it drew shouts of obscenity from the crowded bar. I bent over and felt sick in utter shock, haunting shame, masked guilt, and familial disgrace. This world did not appeal to my strong sense of honoring my father and my mother. Without judging the young lady and the man, I knew I was terribly far out of my element. What was I witnessing? What was I becoming? How have I betrayed my Judeo-Christian ethics? Why did my dreams lead me to this kind of unsettling scene? When would I realize that I could be at a point of NO RETURN? After all the childhood prayers, teen bible studies, lifetime of church gathering, Sunday school studies, anointed singing, choir directing and daily vacation bible school in the summers, punctuated by hymn singing, gospel choir leading, church cookouts and other aspects of my faith-filled life, what was I becoming? Where was I headed? I now realized that I had fallen into the hands of a mortal enemy that soon would wrap me in such spiritual deceit, tie me in such emotional defeat, choke me with such mental disgrace that this EVIL one also known as satan soon would DESTROY my life's path and purpose. John 10:10. I shook in my shoes!

That scene with that male and female in that position in that bar in that section of lower Manhattan shocked me into the reality of the sin-sick soul that I saw in the mirror. I spoke quite briefly to my homegirl. I asked her how she could stand to work in a place that did not represent how she had been reared in Big Texas. She reminded me that she was NOT doing what the dancer was doing and that the money was good. I, however, could see in her countenance that she too was ashamed of the choice she made to earn money as a cocktail waitress in this lewd establishment. My date and I looked at each other and he asked me if I were ready to go. I snatched my handbag as if it were contaminated and headed for the sidewalk. This bar went from one city street straight through to another with both entrances open to the public. Both my date and I in just a few minutes in this place became sickened by the shock by the vulgarity we witnessed among two dear souls. We both glared at the gawking and guffawing of the business attired, inebriated men salivating at their tables, screaming wildly at the muscle bound man's motions under this black draped covering. God, I felt so miserably vulnerable. I felt undressed by these boisterous rounds of lust filled shouts of affirmation for this tastelessly dangerous, money making behavior by this tall, skinny, blank starred dead panned nameless woman. I have no right to judge these dear souls. Admittedly, I do find the behavior entirely undesirable because it objectifies women and dismisses intimacy's power.

When I caught my sister friend's attention one last time, I stared at her shiny black, shiny lacy, body clinging leotard with flapping fringe across the bustline–all accentuated by her black lace hose hugging her thighs, calves and ankles as her 3 inch black suede high heels snuggled her feet. She had already earned a ridiculous sum of money for her rent in just one week. I understood that, but at what cost? Not a cost that I could pay. I cringed at the sight of my dear friend and wanted to wave a magic wand and cause her to "poof" disappear from this whole scene.

In the context of a Christian worldview, my current status with God was as a back slider, one who strayed far away from God after having established a relationship with God. I, now, had become this person who abandoned God even after accepting Christ as Savior. Instead of remaining on a path to transformation, I now deserted that path and followed my will, my way. Having followed Christ's way safely until the traumatic betrayal experience during the two weeks before my graduation from Fisk University, I now headed down a dismal path of disparity. When I reviewed my Christian worldview, I realized I still felt insecure and uncertain about my worth because of the emotional distress of an unfaithful boyfriend, compounded by the betrayal of a cherished female college classmate and running buddy. If you haven't read it already, the full account of this incident is in the book. Nonetheless, I now found myself no longer so much disillusioned with God, but in so many ways–disillusioned with the realities of life. For a fleeting moment, I considered earning all the money that this establishment would yield. Suddenly the stark and cold reality of what I observed in that bar with those after hours businessmen in that community in NYC quickened in me a NEED to change my ways–revisit my own desires and seek God now.

If I did not want to revisit my own upbringing in the Christian church, surely I needed to explore other spiritual and religious world views. Somehow, regarding my own faith background, I convinced myself that I could never get back into God's good graces because of what my eyes witnessed in that bar. I retreated once again from the practice of the Judeo-Christian ethics as well as the application of biblical principles in my life. I had begun to engage in worldly pleasures with some semblance of morality, I thought; and, decent, I thought, self-affirming activities with family and friends around and about New York.

I, however, did not want to go as far as working in this bar either as a waitress or a dancer, not even to earn NYC rent money. This experience became central for me in making the tough decision to stare into the mirror of my soul and determine the path of my future. That experience so horrified me. I noticed that my dear friend had become quite irritable over the months of our friendship. She seemed edgy all the time. Her long flowing black wavy hair that graced her light skinned European features with her piercing, bright and light-brown eyes all seemed diminished by an atmosphere in which she earned her rent money, but was losing so much of herself. I knew that she hated what she was doing. Surely she must have been light years away from the childhood teachings of her family. I already knew that she and I had so much in common. For me in a very personal way, I knew that the prayers of my Daddy and mom would catch up with me and slam dunk me into making an about face from the way that I was living in New York. Indeed the kind of work that I could succumb to in New York to earn money and remain flexible for casting calls, tryouts, rehearsals and all other related activities to the world of theater and music, no longer dominated my life. I, finally, made the decision to search way down deep in my soul and examine the terrifying hold that darkness had on my life during those five years that I walked away from God.

I began this story by sharing with you the beautiful apartment in which I lived in NYC. On that fateful day when I stood in the center of my living room apartment, I heard the voice of God as well as I can hear myself call my name: God said,"come, I have need of thee!" I, then, accepted that my NYC experience faced a final curtain. My beloved, patient, kind and wonderful boyfriend could take a bow, but could not go any further with me. My colleagues in theater could bid me Godspeed but would not choose the path ahead for me. I knew that Broadway stardom evaporated like blowing bubbles at a child's birthday party. A recording contract eluded me like the fight for desegregation in so many places in the southern region of the USA. Paying rent in NYC ended in June 1977. I tearfully left behind my neighbors and friends my lovely and fast growing plants. My luscious, thriving, colorful plants refreshed my life every single day. I left behind my furnishings in the basement of my apartment building with every intention of having them sent to my new residence, once I had one, in Chicago, Illinois. I decided to join Operation PUSH and the Reverend Jesse Louis Jackson, Sr., and fight for human rights as well as equity and parity across this world. Farewell New York City! I decided that some things I cannot, will not, must not do to pay your RENT. Sigh!

Fervent Faith

But without faith it is impossible to please him: for
he that cometh to God must believe that he is, and
that he is a rewarder of them that diligently seek
him. Hebrews 11:6—King James Version

In the final words of Book I of my transformational story, perhaps you will find that I repeat some thoughts from previous chapters. Clearly, the repetition reminds me, as I remind the reader, of how the power and authority of God transformed a life of multiple missteps, frustrating mess ups, and agonizing mistakes into a life of purposeful living in America. God then added fulfilling missionary assignments in several different regions of the world. My fervent faith, saturated in scripture, buoyed me into experiences with women, men and children that arrested me emotionally as well as spiritually. My fervent faith, practiced in all circumstances, sustained me when I failed to work through some of my internal conflicts without such a dramatic expression of them. My fervent faith, edified as I witnessed miracles, catapulted me into unimaginable places and refreshing spaces.

After a five year period of rebellious behavior—resisting God's word, will and way, I submitted to God. These past nearly forty-five years of following the path of the Savior resulted in internal peace. God's perfect love healed my lacerated spirit from the constant rejections at auditions for roles in both Broadway and off-Broadway musicals. God's perfect love healed my bruised heart after one failed romantic relationship and then another. God's perfect love healed my fractured emotions from the insecurities about my birth, my family background, my socio-economic status and my self-esteem. I am a fully recovered, refreshed, and released soul who can now deflect rejection, recognize feigned affection, love unconditionally and serve the needs of the human family in absolute confidence that God's perfect love will strengthen me. While I remain imperfect as a member of the human family, God's perfection boosts my confidence and inspires me to go forth in this transformed self that I fully embrace.

Fervent faith occurs when the scriptures become actualized in your life. I needed to experience *Matthew 6:33*, "…God would add all other things if I did seek the kingdom of God first"; *Philippians 4:19*, "…God would supply my needs according to his riches in glory"; *I Corinthians 10:13*, "…God would not allow me to be tempted above that which I could stand, but would with the temptation make a way of escape"; *Psalm 23*, "…God would make me lie down in green pastures, restore my soul, prepare a table before me in the presence of my enemies"; *John 15:1*, "…God would allow me to experience fruit from my labor as I remained in God." As I studied the scriptures, I then realized the biblical principles and

Judeo-Christian ethics in my daily life. I needed confirmation that God's word works. I needed to experience it in real time. I wanted to see God's word actualized in my life. It happened. I did see it. I experienced the above scriptures in real time and I still experience them. What an explosion of confidence in my spirit when my daddy's God and my mom's God became my God. Way down deep in my soul, I needed to know this God: Creator, Redeemer, Sustainer of life.

Before I experienced fervent faith, I trusted my intuition, my extensive education, and my lived experiences to satisfy my inner longings. All of the aforementioned failed me in some measure—so much so—that I had an itch I could not scratch. My intuition, my education, my lived experiences and above all, my personality failed to gratify my nagging lack of internal peace. I just knew that my personality that put people at ease would win the day. It did not. I felt discounted over and over again. In fact, I recall the days in my life when my vivacious personality cost me friends. Some folks considered a steady diet of my "love child" behavior impractical. Thankfully, through Christian counseling, I discovered those who actually welcomed my company as opposed to those who simply accommodated me.

People pleasing cost me significant productivity in my life. Even now, I repent before God for the years that I earnestly sought the approval of dearly beloved folks. I finally turned over to God the need to reinvent myself—on demand—to satisfy some dear souls in my family, profession, community or church. I am now living to please God and God alone. Actually, God is much easier to please than humans. I now love the human family up close and personal as well as from a distance. God taught me how to manage my deep longing to be accepted by folks. I try to warmly accept everyone. I pray to see people for the unique ways in which God created them. Nonetheless, authenticity matters to me—I, therefore, work earnestly to be sincere with my fellow humans. Love finds a way to work through painful conflicts in human relationships. I've found it so. God pours perfect love into broken vessels and we then pour God's perfect love into others. When you find repetitions in this book, two things occurred—my zeal exceeded wisdom in my proofreading; and I tend to overstate my presentation of a life transformed by God's perfect love. I struggled for decades trusting God to find romantic love, marriage and the family. After the most demanding struggle in my seminary days, I finally accepted my single status. I then allowed God to fill my life to overflowing with God's patience, joy, forgiveness, gentleness, meekness, long suffering, reconciliation and every aspect of the character of Christ in my relationships with others. My imperfections loomed large in my estimation. I, however, received responses that affirmed me as a loving person.

Thank God I did not fail God. That mattered more than anything to me. In this way, I appreciate your patience as you read some duplications in this book. Let's continue.

Because I discovered that God works in and through our personalities, *I titled my book God's Love: Extravagant Evidence.* As a teen, I discovered that I possessed a vivacious personality—animated, friendly, high energy and cheerful extending my hand to strangers. Effusive in my compliments—nonetheless, genuinely admiring gifts, possessions, and the aesthetics of others—I discovered that some folks resisted my personality—maybe they were curious about my sincerity. Perhaps some of the push back occurred due to regional differences. I came of age in southern culture—even in southwestern San Antonio. In my early twenties, I relocated to the northeastern region of the country. I confess, New Yorkers' ways of doing things and my personality style did not sync for a while—a long while. I think I made my way around Washington, DC fairly well, but there too, my sophistication or lack thereof, seemed glaring to me.

I also lived in the midwest, in Chicago, for several years. There, I found greater acceptance of my southern charm and welcoming disposition. I found that the windy city received migrants from Tennessee, Arkansas, North and South Carolina and Georgia among other states. Across those regions, sometimes folks thought of me as expressive, even overly expressive. Others sometimes misunderstood my vivacious personality. I remember when one professor in my seminary experience in New Jersey told me: "It takes some getting used to your personality." I kept thinking that might not be a compliment. Perhaps by his words he meant that my personality seemed unreal or unbelievable, maybe! I guess I'm still not sure just what that esteemed professor meant by such words. Pressing on, I believe God has shown me extravagant evidence of God's perfect love. Temperance prevents some misunderstandings.

I suspect that I desired to express such love to others. Sometimes expressing love—warmth, concern, care, interest, compassion—to others lands in the heart of those who question your motive. The chapters in this book offer some evidence of the unusual experiences of my life that I attribute to extravagant evidence of God's love. When I have the opportunity to share with others, I tell them story after story of the extravagant evidence of God's love in my checkered life; the circuitous routes I traveled that landed me smack in the middle of the hands of God. Having celebrated my thirtieth birthday, I longed for the table of my life to completely turn—centering me in my purpose. From that July day in 1977 to the present hour, I seek to digest more and more of the scriptures, to follow Christ, to love aloud as I—affirm others, care for children, attend to widows, share my resources, support charitable causes, smile at strangers—living more intentionally according to both the scriptures and the Holy Spirit's guidance. Everyone has access to God's perfect love because, I believe, that God is the Creator, Redeemer, and Sustainer of life. God has shown me such extravagant evidence of unconditional love that it compelled me to become a totally transformed creature. In my battle of wills with God, I wish that I had surrendered my will ten years earlier. Once I released my personality completely to God for melting, molding, shaping and making me into a vessel of honor for God, I anticipated incomparable joy. In this way, I settled myself, quieted my spirit, sat before God on a daily basis and received this infilling of God's love. It comes every day in ways that shake me and stir up my emotions. It checks me like a chess kingpin. It directs my path. Yes!

Vivacious personality or not, God's love compelled me to selflessly love others without expectations. I keep trying to make that a daily practice in my life. When I miss the mark, I try again and thank God for another opportunity. Love is not silly, giddy, weak, pathetic, namby, pamby tossed around slogans and sentiments. Love is a tough, demanding, diligent, and daring work from sunrise to sunset every day of my life. Love is clearly the work of the supernatural. In a Christian context, we call this supernatural work the leading of the paraclete, the Holy Spirit. Jesus, before he ascended into heaven, graciously left in the earth realm—the Holy Spirit—for strength, guidance, courage and power for his followers. The more I look to the Holy Spirit to guide me through all circumstances, the more I experience victory even in disappointment, struggles, and catastrophic events in my life. I thank God that surrender, submission and obedience keep me healthy holistically. In the absence of God's love, I believe that I would be an embittered American citizen spewing cynicism, indifference, and judgments. I believe that my caustic tongue would cut and create unnecessary hurt in the lives of others. I suspect I would seek revenge for what did happen to me. I believe that anger and hostility would be my signature regarding what did not happen for me that I believed I deserved. Who am I to decide that I should have a path of ease? What makes me think that I deserved or earned such blessings from our great God? In all of this, God refreshes me daily with his overwhelming love. The constant reminder comes when I move in and out of all kinds of circumstances with precious people who care about my well being.

Because my behavior, anchored in southern culture, reflects a flair for warm, hospitable acceptance of others, I must look to the Holy Spirit to guide me to wholesome relationships of God's choosing and not my own. In my idealism, I sometimes become an incurable romanticist—as my mom would always say: "…looking at the world through rose colored glasses." My mom and dad prayed unceasingly that God's hand would help me to accept the things I could not change. Believing in God, reading the bible, going to church all the time, studying the Judeo-Christian ethics and biblical principles—taught and modeled by my parents, neighbors and church leaders during my developmental years—left a healthy fingerprint on my soul. My on-going involvement in music and the arts improved my sometimes overly sensitive responses to teasing; and, my misinterpretation of others' behavior toward me. I memorized a hit song that told me I only needed LOVE. I committed to finding love in a romantic context, seeking to give such love to family and friends, and longing to share it far and near. I struggled to accept that Jesus is love and yet Jesus was crucified. Martin Luther King, Jr. espoused love, demonstrated its capacity to effect social change and yet he was assassinated. I wondered if I made an idol out of love. I needed everyone to respond to my love for them. I tended to gush about it. Some shied away. Still others questioned it.

In my early childhood and teen years, I wondered if my personality pleased God. I observed those in Sunday School, bible study, worship services and other church related activities with calm, composed, quiet and compliant personalities. I thought maybe their personalities were more angelic because in many ways, my personality traits differed distinctly from theirs. I asked myself, would God love me more if I had a more compliant, quiet, soft-spoken, disposition? I earned the title of "princess" from my playmates and teen sister friends. I always wanted to be the main character in the plays, the leader in the groups, and "the boss" of the children. Though I loved everyone, I needed to be in the center of things to feel their love in return. I noticed that this enigmatic and sometimes immature behavior did not always win friends.

As an active and chatty student in school, my mom cautioned me about backtalk. She reminded me that instruction from my teachers and other adults required a polite response. Though my mom respected my inquiry with her regarding all things, she knew that I could be misunderstood in school and other settings. I always needed more explanation and that resulted in my asking why? This one word often resulted in teachers disciplining me by having me write 100 times: "I will not talk in our classroom!" In southern culture and in the Jim Crow south, backtalk received a stern rebuke from adults. Backtalk in African-American culture in some families could get you a backhand lick from those family members who came of age during World War I. My parents wanted their children to guard their tongue and hold some of their thoughts for their diaries. Backtalk suggested that you disrespected the status of the elders.

Teachers for many baby boomers received the kind of treatment athletes and entertainers receive in the 21st century. My teachers received a measure of hero worship. They attracted attention like the super stars of social media today. When we encountered them in the marketplace, we felt honored to exchange pleasantries with them. In some ways, our teachers were revered because many of them practiced high moral conduct and set admirable examples in the community. They received the utmost respect. I collided with one teacher while an 8th grade student at Douglass Junior High School. I loved social studies, but I did not think that this teacher loved me or any of her students. In my experience, she offered a rigid hand and a facial scowl most days. I sensed that this dear teacher provided instruction with a voice that sounded more like that of an impatient dog trainer. Where was the love I wondered. Why didn't she sound more like she loved us as her students? One day she had taken enough of my sassy remarks. She sent me to the principal's office. That day my mom was contacted. She knew the principal and his family through his kid sister who happened to be our neighbor. If he had spoken with his sister, a lovely teacher herself, he would have known that my mom and dad were God-fearing, upright citizens deeply committed to instilling in their children respect for authority figures. Well, this dear principal said something horrific to my mom. He told her that he thought she must have been a tramp to have a daughter that spoke out of turn like me. WHAT? Where was the love? I decided then that if ever I became a teacher—and in fact I did—I would NEVER tell a parent that I thought less of him or her because of the behavior of his/her son or daughter that I taught. My smart mouth did not reflect my home training. My smart mouth reflected my recoiling at the absence of love. For some reason, this particular teacher ignored my love. That disturbed my peace.

Later that evening at home, my mom and daddy needed to process with me the behavior that led to a telephone call by a principal who offended my mom. My daddy looked at me as if to say: "Where did you come from?" My mom said that she felt it unfair that the principal used such harsh terms to characterize our homelife and my mom's social status. We needed to work through that discussion for a little while. That incident became the backdrop for a number of discussions to come—except that I did not back talk to any more teachers after that, not ever.

From my perspective as a 13 year old, I thought that I reacted normally to the absence of love in my teacher's treatment of me and my classmates. I simply did not know how to handle the matter. Besides, I have since learned that I should have questioned the kind of love as a 13 year old that I showed my teachers.

Could my love be considered entirely conditional? Perhaps I appeared to be a needy student—needing NOT to be ignored ever. Sigh.

As a strong-willed, curious, adventure seeking love child, I needed my mom and dad's unyielding arm of correction and gentle guidance to stay out of conflicts where I talked too much. In my mind, I just expressed myself. I did not know it then, but later I learned that I had a "queen complex." Now the "queen complex" is definitely another story for a different book. Suffice to say, I not only needed to love and be loved in return, but also to be served by others. Fortunately, in both junior high and high school, I received royal treatment from many male suitors—all of whom had to face my parents and older brother's scrutiny before they could visit with me in our home. I suspect I not only watched too many 19th century romance movies, but also read too many 19th century romance novels and tried to live vicariously through them. I digress.

Chicago Conversion

But seek ye first the kingdom of God, and his righteousness; and all these things shall be added unto you. Matthew 6:33—King James Version

I settled myself soaking up the sun, feeling the comfy, colorful surroundings in my apartment on West 86th Street in my cherished New York City. I lingered before the window recalling the days of my apartment dweller lifestyle. Musing, I smiled broadly at the bustle along the sidewalks as pedestrians hustled to the subway station just a the corner block from my door. As I gazed in awe upon the beauty of the blue skies covering the tall, swaying limbs on the grandiose trees in my neighborhood just a few hundred feet from Central Park West, I knew that I soon would relocate to Chicago, Illinois. Alas, though saddened, I accepted my fate. In a few days, as I recognized that bidding farewell to New York City involved a significant change in my destiny, I tried to think positively. Suddenly overwhelmed by thoughts of what fortune may be found in Chicago, I pushed myself to pack, pursuing a new path for my life.

Reflecting upon several years spent stomping the grounds and chasing my dreams to be in theater, I actually found relief in my soon exit. I earnestly desired to sign publishing contracts with record companies in New York; but, I suddenly lost the taste to continue "to beg!" In this way, I abandoned my hopes for stardom in the theater or film; relinquished my hopes for an offer to record my voice; and accepted the possibility of a new world. Though my heart ached because I had finally earned my Actor's Equity membership, I knew my New York season had a termination date. Such disappointment gripped me when I realized I may never get to use my Actor's Equity card in a union production. This coveted union card allowed serious actors greater access to casting calls and a more hopeful opportunity to be signed by a talent agency. So, what do you do when your dreams begin to dissipate like blown up birthday candles—the smoke fades, the cake is eaten, the residue of a great celebration now lingers only in your mind and maybe great photos. The party was over.

Alas, I placed most of my earthly goods in the basement of my apartment building with the "gentleman's agreement" between my landlord and me that I would have them shipped to my new home in the coming weeks. I prayed that my landlord would not be unkind and sell my goods for his personal profit. My landlord's god was money and more money. Within the first two weeks after I traveled from New York to Chicago, I discovered through the switchboard operator in my apartment building, that my landlord betrayed me. The switchboard operator, named Davie, was an immigrant from South America with whom I exchanged pleasantries often. Davie told me that he knew that our landlord had sold my beautiful furnishings because, in fact, Davie bought many of the items. Rather than engage Davie in a moral and integrity dialogue, I suffered the loss as further evidence of the betrayal and deceit that colored my life over the past eight years following my graduation from Fisk University. In spite of my stunning disappointment that I must now pay for furniture that someone else bought from my landlord, I welcomed a radical change in my existence. Pursuing inner peace rushed to the top of my "to do" list. Peace must now occupy a place of prominence, prevailing in my perplexed psyche.

Arriving in Chicago became surrealistic for the first few hours. Lover of water that I am, the city's lakefront captured my attention. I wondered about the possibility of living in a lakefront apartment. My first week in Chicago, I spent with a friend. Though I scarcely knew this dear soul, I appreciated her warm hospitality. Toni, my hostess, possessed a joyful, bubbly personality that enhanced her pretty, bright eyed, silky smooth light skinned face. I quickly learned that Toni had an occult fetish. She entered deeply into occult activities evidenced by her impending wedding plans. Toni scrutinized the numerological charts, the astrological charts and the place of the sun, and thereby arrived at a wedding date for herself and her fiance. She shared with me that this dear man seemed suitable to her family and her lifestyle. Accordingly, wedding plans permeated the atmosphere in Toni's home. Such plans needed to be designed and executed to the specifications of the numerological, astrological and sun dial for safe harbor in the impending ceremonial rites.

I felt uneasy about Toni's proceedings because I left a lifestyle in New York of tinkering and tottering with the occult. I mastered the skill of palmistry and worked closely with my friend who practiced Tarot Card readings, numerology and astrology. She served many clients. Unbelievably, nothing consumed more of my time than the occult. After production rehearsals, voice lessons and work, then the mysterious world of the occult and its amazing effects on the lives of my fellow thespians and clients charged my evening and weekend hours.

Now, here I find myself, first thing in Chicago in the thick of the occult in a friend's home where these practices governed every detail of her proposed marriage and family plans. For me, this seemed such a strange occurrence since I longed for a new way of thinking, walk-ing, talking and living. Perhaps this experience presented to me my first real test of sincerity. I shared in the final preparations for Toni's wedding, enjoyed meeting her family, romanticized about love, marriage and the family during the actual ceremony and soon after concluded that I would seek more permanent housing accommoda-tions. I landed a delightful room in the five-bedroom home of an Operation PUSH staff member. The house on Chicago's southside was quite lovely, spacious, and situated in a quiet and well-manicured community of homeowners. I loved my large, airy room and thought that it would serve my purposes for at least the first few months in Chicago.

My initial plans to become engaged in social activism in Chicago took me to the Operation People United to Serve Humanity [PUSH] headquarters. I expected to receive some spiritual food in my voluntary service and in the life of the PUSH family. After all, I lived with one of the staff members. I recalled an occasion in New York, when I met Reverend Jesse Louis Jackson, Sr., his press secretary, Reverend Frank Watkins, and his International Affairs Director, Jack O'Dell. That encounter, though short-lived—focused upon a typing assignment that later beckoned me to the Operation People United to Serve Humanity [PUSH] family. Little did I know that a simple typing assignment became my entry into training to become a human rights activist. God strategically placed me in the care of two women with Operation PUSH who had already gained national and international prominence for their civil rights leadership.

These two women ignited my transformation experience. I sensed that my destiny with these two women: Reverend Dr. Willie Taplin Barrow at Operation PUSH and Reverend Dr. Addie Wyatt, International Vice President of the United Food and Commercial Workers Union, offered a brighter professional, social and spiritual future than I could imagine. I, therefore, not only volunteered to sing in the choir and to assist the Rev. Barrow at Operation PUSH, but also I volunteered to assist Rev. Addie with the multiple details of her "many hats wearing" lifestyle. I counted on Frank Watkins at PUSH to guide me through the path to becoming an effective volunteer at PUSH. He worked graciously with me.

After I ended my first professional job in Chicago that required significant travel, I landed a second job at the Chicago Urban League. Some evenings and all Saturdays, I sang in the PUSH choir at our rousing PUSH meetings informing and inspiring action in human rights affairs both nationally and internationally. In Chicago, I experienced my greatest joy when I spent Sundays at Vernon Park Church of God, under the leadership of Pastor Claude L. Wyatt and Co-Pastor Addie Wyatt. Rev. Barrow and Rev. Addie committed to my spiritual growth and development. They embraced me as a daughter and nurtured me during my tenure with Vernon Park. I enjoyed the company of a group of dedicated believers at Vernon Park who taught me how to cultivate an intercessory prayer life. My personal friendships with Jimmy, Nona and Tijuana Orr rounded out the family fulfillment of my life in Chicago.

Once persons who served in civic and human rights groups and planned programs learned of my singing talents, I accepted many invitations to sing for Civil Rights rallies. Forging friendships with

Ron and Queenie Musten along with several other couples as well as Chicago local activists brought me countless hours of joy as they imparted to me the tenets of imperialism and its world dominance. I became a student of a few different ideologies regarding the cause for justice and human rights worldwide. I studied the tenets of men and women from the 20th century who authored texts that acquainted me with strategies for liberation and freedom in our own nation and across the world. My eyes were opened wide to the ways in which oppression subdued members of the human family across the globe. I wanted to participate in breaking the chains of oppression. I knew that my vocal talents warmed the souls of listeners. I just knew that I now found my niche. I skipped along, sensing renewed hope in my dreams.

I began to articulate how oppression reduced the chances of potential leaders, talents, and brilliance from occurring in so many different countries. The bloodshed by those who resisted oppression and fought for liberation humbled me to such an extent that my body often would grow limp during the discussions. Both provocation and evocation permeated my singing style and punctuated my passionate performances at liberation rallies. In Chicago I connected with two women artists. Peggy Lipschutz, a chalk talk artist and Becky Armstrong, a guitarist, folk singer and composer. As a classically trained vocalist who could sing gospel, I joined these two gifted women. We three—one black, one Scottish, one Jewish—came together in a group called "Songs You Can See." We began to perform for both union and women's events and received multiple invitations in our short tenure together. Both Peggy and Rebecca's marriages hit turbulence in the years of our time together. Such turbulence required them to rearrange their lifestyles. I floundered somewhat seeking stability in employment and even returning to the university setting to improve my skill set. Over the years, I learned that both Peggy Lipschutz and Rebecca Armstrong went on to noteworthy success in their quarter of a century of working together. I so longed for the day that we could all three reunite. It never happened. The question of why haunted me for sometime.

These two women and I seemed perfectly suited to one another. We enjoyed the commonality of artistry, justice, freedom and liberation advocacy, and social activism. Why, God, why did you not let this work for me? These women were beautiful in spirit, bountiful in service, and blessed in talent and convictions. Nonetheless, we did not share the love of Jesus Christ as the dominating source of our joy and purpose. This truth filled my heart with sorrow. Perhaps I could negotiate with God and get around some issues with Peggy and Rebecca. NO, there is no getting around the issue of God's will, God's word, God's way for individual lives. I knew that I could not keep my left foot on the soil of my will and my right foot on the soil of God's will. Sinking in the misery of trying to live a double life, shocked me into the world of singular living. I now must either go all the way with God or all the way with my way! I chose to go all the way with God.

My new life in Chicago seemed well suited to fulfill my deep longings for family. I made friends easily and found myself surrounded by a wholesome church family life. I found in God: perfect love. I found in the fellowship of believers, fulfilling emotional and spiritual relationships. Over the months, I, however, brought to this church environment, the seedy residue of my New York City lifestyle and internally I felt UNCLEAN. My feelings manifested in emotional insecurity and edginess in my communications with others. One prayer partner advised me to curve my caustic tongue. That very statement demanded of me something that I possessed little skill to change. I, then, needed God to intercept my hurtful words expressed through agonizing emotions. Spiritual surgery followed in the days ahead. I submitted to deliverance services that allowed you to purge your inner turmoil and free yourself to receive an extreme makeover on Christ Jesus. This makeover occurred through wrestling with the scriptures. As I sought to apply the scriptures to my life intentionally, I gained confidence in my acceptance by God and others.

At Vernon Park Church of God, I trained and conducted a children's choir. I taught them several songs each month. Once a month, our children's choir processed to the sanctuary upstairs from our downstairs children's church services. We then sang for the adult

Sunday worship service. The response to the children on each 4th Sunday thrilled me. I found my place and purpose at Vernon Park Church of God. The children's choir continued to grow and numbered over sixty children, eager to sing and to learn the scriptures. What a complete joy for me.

Thinking through my assignments at Vernon Park with the children's choir and my Wednesday evening prayer and bible study assignment as the musician, I wondered what God planned for me. I studied the scriptures for hundreds of hours now. I listened to hours of bible studies that taught scripture exegesis. I participated in hours of prayer. I landed on my feet after some turbulence with the polity of my church. I insisted on learning as much about God's way and I now found myself totally surrendered. I remained more than confident that some dear soul will profit from the aspects of this story with which he or she resonates and will find in God alone: perfect love, marriage, and the family. I have yet to do so. I shall never give up. I continue to believe.

This story chronicles a series of events in the life of one woman who understood early in her life that she wanted profoundly fulfilling love, blissful marriage and a joy filled, adventure seeking family life. These three she determined would cause her life to have purpose, pleasure and productivity. Of the three items listed above, I only found to date the profoundly fulfilling and perfect love of God. Undoubtedly, I would not be the woman that I am today without the unspeakable joy of God's love. I have seen eye widening, jaw dropping, "wow after wow" of God's love for me through such extravagant EVIDENCE in my health, visions, pursuits, and relationships. My soul is happy in the Lord. I still believe God for the other two items aforementioned. God has a time, place and space in my life for blissful marriage and faithful family life. I shall patiently await his arrangements in confidence.

Just think, It all began on a sunny afternoon in Los Angeles, California on the parking lot of a church where our 1977 PUSH Convention occurred. One simple question challenged me: "Have you considered this scripture: Seek ye first the kingdom of God and God's righteousness, then all other things will be added unto it.

Matthew 6:33" [My paraphrase] Clearly, I had not considered that scripture. I decided on that sunny Saturday in that church parking lot in LA to allow that scripture to wash over my entire soul and guide me to the truth of God's transforming power through his son Jesus Christ. I found it to be true. Nothing comforted me more than this truth: I could become a new creature—this I wanted more than anything else in this world.

Thank you for reading this story and sharing it with someone you love.

Racial Reconciliation

And all things are of God, who hath reconciled us to himself by Jesus Christ, and hath given to us the ministry of reconciliation; To wit, that God was in Christ, reconciling the world unto himself, not imputing their trespasses unto them; and hath committed unto us the word of reconciliation
II Corinthians 5:18-19—King James Version

From 1977 to 1983, my eyes were opened to see the reality of racially inflamed relations between blacks and white. Because I learned all about my Intelligence Quotient [IQ] in high school, I sometimes felt anxious about competing academically with white students. Though I graduated from high school in 1965, with fewer than 5% of my class made up of white students, my teachers were all white. I often wondered if they believed in the mental acuity of their black and brown students. They certainly believed in our creative and athletic talents. They saw plenty of evidence of such gifts among us.

Nonetheless, I found myself in Chicago in 1977 witnessing blatant racially inflamed experiences in the Chicago Public School system, the housing opportunities, shopping on the Magnificent Mile, and in private industry's hiring patterns. Suddenly, I wondered if my average IQ may cause me some professional difficulties in Chicago. The word average triggered stifling thoughts of limitations. Standing on the sidewalks in The Loop in Chicago, I reflected upon my thoughts as a 1965 high school graduate having learned of my average IQ. I had graduated a second time since high school. I earned my college degree, became an independent adult in both New York City and Washington, DC, discovered that I had the capacity to master academic content in institutions of higher education, learned of my vocal talents, identified my creative energies and yet I struggled with insecurity because of that silly form that showed I had an average IQ.

What fears did I face in Chicago? Why would I now begin to rehearse my socio-economic status as a black female with an average IQ from a working class/middle class family? Perhaps relocating to Chicago without a relative or friend there caused me second thoughts. I began to think through how I could navigate opportunities for higher education, directions for a career path, and avenues to becoming a homeowner? I decided to volunteer at Operation PUSH to determine what I could offer to their cause. I found no disappointment there. My experiences at Operation PUSH answered my prayers. As an unknown to the Operation PUSH staff and family, and without any contacts there, I managed to move through the organization with ease and acceptance. What a privilege. The PUSH staff identified housing accommodations and employment for me within a few days of my association with them. My life in Chicago began on a high note.

I reflected upon my years between college graduation and my arrival at PUSH. I decided that just because my matriculation at the University of Pittsburgh and my subsequent pursuit of theatrical contracts did not quite materialize, I should not count those missteps as a death sentence. I questioned myself: "what caused this sudden shrinking of confidence in Chicago?" Perhaps it reminded me of what I thought we as a people had overcome. In Chicago in the late 70's, I found racially charged reactions in the marketplace, doors closed in some business and private industry spaces, glass ceilings for blacks and women, protests in communities against blacks moving into their neighborhoods and even violent reactions to black people—all of which triggered in me painful memories of the Jim Crow south in which I came of age. I could not believe that I had read—and now realizing a reality—a play written in the 50's by a gifted female playwright about a black family purchasing a home in a white neighborhood in Chicago and being offered money to stay out. We were now in the late 70's and black families were encountering violence in some white neighborhoods where they chose to purchase a home. Triggers and more triggers negatively affected my confidence in my own capacity to overcome. Nonetheless, Operation PUSH offered serious action against injustice and inspired me to fight against racial oppression.

Suddenly all that I faced in the Jim Crow south; the words by the white high school counselor spoken to me about becoming a beautician by attending the colored beauty school; the inability to grasp the concepts of geometry; the frustrations with physics—all these thoughts flooded by mind as I stood on the corner of Michigan Avenue and Harrison Street in Chicago. Suddenly I realized that my previous choices and even failures were not the final word for my destiny. I summoned the strength of my mom and Granny. I resonated with their words—"CarolAnn, you are not limited by your southern roots nor the experiences of high school. You must learn to refuse the word NO as the final answer." My mom demonstrated that she achieved her goals because she simply would not take no for a final answer. My grandmother challenged me to take the word "can't" out of my vocabulary. She told me never again to tell her what I can't do. She promised me that if I tried, God would guide me and show me how I can do what I must do to succeed. I needed to gather my wits in Chicago. I determined that my dad's prayers, my mom's drive and my grandparents' strong sense of what they could do through their faith in God must now become my complete foundation for going forward in Chicago. My grandparents and parents believed in me. Now, I must learn to believe in myself. Fearing that I would disappoint our family legacy, I settled myself in Chicago confident that I could achieve my goals there.

In this way, my average IQ concerns bumped into the brilliant mind of the Rev. Jesse Louis Jackson, Sr. I recalled my quick and amazing encounter with Rev. Jackson and several of his staff members some years earlier in New York City. That typing assignment gave me the chutzpah to march through the doors at Operation PUSH in Chicago and advise the staff that I came there to volunteer. Though I did not have the pedigree, that is, I neither had a civil rights record of achievements, nor did I obtain a law degree, but I had a strong will to produce and a good mind to learn. Because I belonged to a critical thinking community in New York, I learned to defend, qualify, explain and advance my ideas through sound reasoning. So, I decided to share my ideas in response to Rev. Jackson's messages. Often, I passed a hand-written note scratched out on a jagged torn edge of paper from my notebook. My words to him provided both feedback and direction regarding a speech I heard from Rev. Jackson in a regularly scheduled rally on Saturday morning at our Drexel Boulevard Operation PUSH headquarters. I took immense pride in sharing my thoughts with Rev. Jackson, believing them to be both progressive and reflective of his message. Rev. Jackson graciously responded to me. Occasionally I encountered him in the corridors of our PUSH building and he would say: "I got your note. I'm thinking about what you shared." Wow, I thought, Rev. Jesse Louis Jackson, Sr. read the notes that I wrote to him sharing my ideas about what needed to happen with our plans for liberation, how the course of events could be charted, and the strong sense of direction that I thought we should take. Imagine that I tried to tell Rev. Jackson what I thought could happen and why regarding our plans to stir up in the nation a need to be just, earnest and to respond to our cries for liberation. What did I really know? I certainly knew how to talk and to think as well. I sit in amazement today when I think of the kind gesture that this civil rights leader showed to me.

In the late 70's and early 80's, Saturday morning rallies at PUSH brought to our platform national and international political leaders, business women and men, entertainers, educators and anyone who wished to align with Operation PUSH. Such persons demonstrated a commitment to seeking justice, advancing policies, guaranteeing equity and parity in the marketplace and addressing human rights issues globally. Rev. Jackson, himself a national and international Human Rights leader became one of the often quoted voices of the 70's and 80's. He addressed socio-economic, educational, political and systemic injustices in the whole of Chicago and across the USA. Rev. Jackson aligned with international leaders on the continent of Africa. He forged relationships with activist groups representing oppressive conditions in Central America, South America and other regions of the world. Growing numbers of corporate leaders, business owners, elected officials, entrepreneurs, entertainers, athletes and the "rag tag motley crew"of everyday people joined forces to address the nation's need for appropriate action to repair America's social, political and economic infrastructure.

Employed by the Chicago Urban League, I served in a professional capacity over several years with a variety of programs including the ESAA, [Emergency School Aid Act, a desegregation program]; CETA,[Comprehensive Training and Employment Act, a job training for the disadvantaged]; and the LEAP, [Labor Education Advancement Program, an opportunity for minorities in the construction trades]; that allowed me to both earn a living and confront issues of inequity. In retrospect, I wish I could now examine the research, the statistics, the data and the demographics to discern the cumulative effect of these several above named programs. The bloodshed and violence in Chicago, perceivably unmatched worldwide, brings to mind the unrelenting efforts by Operation PUSH, OIC [Opportunities Industrialization Corporation, Rev. Leon Sullivan's vision]; the National Urban League, SCLC [Southern Christian Leadership Conference]; and a host of other organizations, agencies and activist groups seeking social, political and economic freedom and equality among minorities and women. I remember listening to a world renown folk singer who addressed the causes of the trade unions. Some of this singer's lyrics found roots in the scripture: Ecclesiastes 3:1-8. Those lyrics and principles in the scriptures stimulated richly rewarding dialogues with activists and others longing for change.

I remember singing one of my favorite songs about change on the occasion that we honored Dr. Benjamin Chavis of the Wilmington Ten. The privilege of singing before Dr. Chavis delivered his message, reminding me of how much God loved me gently refreshed my soul. God repeatedly arranged golden opportunities for me to sing before prominent men and women engaged in social justice and human rights struggles. I sang with such conviction familiar union songs recognizing and believing passionately that the union makes us strong. The union protects our workers by providing critical boundaries that all workers must have to sustain an effective work environment. I sang with the celebrated Peggy Lipschutz [Chalk Talk

Artist] and Rebecca Armstrong [Folk Singer and Stringed Instrument Musician] songs of hope, progress, liberation, unity, love and power. Our group: "Songs You Can See" believed in the remarkable power of patriotism to close the gaps among all people groups.

We all belonged to the blood soaked soil of the United States of America. We sang provocative lyrics about our nation's history. I belted those lyrics out with the fortitude of a laborer. I believed in what I sang. I wanted protection and rights for farmers, maritime workers, teachers, janitors, sanitation workers, bus drivers, chauffeurs, shoe shine boys/men, cashiers, butchers, barbers, hair stylists, telephone operators, cleaning crews, EMS crews, etc. I studied the life of Paul Robeson adopting his passion for justice and fierce independence from oppressive governments. I felt inspired to imitate Robeson's passionate renditions of songs that shaped our American culture. The 70's and 80's in American cities like Chicago, New York, and Washington, DC found me singing, marching, protesting, living and learning to be a part of the social/political progress in human rights. I wanted to contribute to the good of the international human rights movement that resounded worldwide. In this way, I still believe in the *Greatest Generation* and the *Baby Boomers* connecting with succeeding generations committed to realize our visions for a renewed America. We have a better world than many previous generations experienced. In these remaining few years of the first quarter of this twenty-first century, our intergenerational efforts can become models for our children and their children.

Church Champions

Worshiping at Vernon Park Church of God became an extension of my Saturday morning jubilance at Operation PUSH rallies. Our church leadership participated directly in much of the "good trouble" at Operation PUSH. In this way, I felt affirmed by the scriptures to confront the immeasurable injustices among oppressed people across the globe. At last, I was living my dream. I participated in the fight for justice. Through my Texas association, I befriended the first

Lieutenant to Rev. Jackson. She wore the title of the "Little Warrior." All of her 4'8' tall frame suited the stunningly beautiful ensembles she wore. She, Rev. Willie Taplin Barrow, was a feisty, dynamic, personable and larger than life figure in Rev. Jackson's operation. She loved her role as his 2nd in command and took her duties quite seriously. In this way, she became a custodian for the young women, such as I, who looked in awe at Rev. Jackson. She befriended me and clearly kept me from any foolish behavior or vain imaginings with Rev. Jackson. She cautioned all of the young women who swooned over Rev. Jackson to stop their foolishness and remember that he was a responsible married man with five children. She sobered up every young woman that thought she should work closely with Rev. Jackson. I am thankful to God that she did that for me.

I counted myself among the most fortunate of women, that Rev. Willie Taplin Barrow, through spiritual discernment, no doubt, redirected my energies to significant voluntary activities that distanced me from close contact with Rev. Jackson. My good fortune provided an opportunity to assist and support the International Affairs Director in the person of Dr. Jack O'Dell who was a delightful personality. We befriended one another and steered clear of any romantic frivolity. In this way, he felt secure in a genuine friendship and we flourished as we worked together on his international affairs activities/projects for several years. Jack O'Dell taught me about the nations of Nigeria, Ghana and Kenya on the continent of Africa. He helped me to understand the growing need that African Americans had to establish productive relationships with not only the leadership of those nations, but also the people. He supplied me with books and other materials and encouraged me to read and learn about the peoples of several African nations. I did and I learned to appreciate the heritage of the black Americans in these United States, the Caribbean, Central and South America as well. Jack O'Dell proved to be a source of significant inspiration for my international travels in the years beyond PUSH. Clearly, he was a trusted friend and mentor.

The Back Story

Before I arrived in Chicago, I had befriended Rev. Jackson's Press Secretary, Rev. Frank Watkins. Over the years, Rev. Watkins served in several different roles on Rev. Jackson's Operation PUSH staff as well as with former Congressman Jesse Jackson, Jr. During Rev. Watkins' Chicago years, he purchased a beautiful home in a lovely community on Chicago's south side. He hosted visitors who needed temporary housing. I was one of them. During our weekend activities at Operation PUSH, I became better acquainted with the duties of Rev. Watkins' role as Press Secretary to Rev. Jackson. I hammered him with many questions. He responded patiently. On one occasion, he shared with me that in a staff meeting, a discussion led to the need to identify a candidate for a new position with a specific project. Someone in the meeting recommended me. I was told that someone objected fiercely to my receiving the position. As the discussion unfolded, I was told that Rev. Jackson stated: "I don't know why you have a problem with Carol. Her mind is razor sharp!"

When Frank Walker told me this, all of my issues related to my average IQ were forever settled in heaven and on earth. As far as I am concerned, on that day, Jesus spoke through Rev. Jackson. My appreciation for Rev. Jackson's statement in that staff meeting regarding my mental acuity considering the insecurities that I had about them became a launching pad for me. I gained such confidence from hearing that Rev. Jackson, whose mind I certainly admired, in both hearing and believing that Rev. Jackson respected my mind—believe it, that was the beginning of cracking a shell of inferiority that plagued me for sometime. It seems as if I dusted myself from the cumulative residue of negative feedback from college professors—just two actually—and frenemies who loved to bully me.

I now face a new day. I began to believe in myself. Of course my parents had spoken thousands of words of life into my spirit. I believed them. Then, lived experiences in academia, the workplace and the community seemed to disturb my sense of productivity. Just those words, from one man's mouth to my ears changed the trajectory of my life. I walked around thinking that I had a razor sharp mind. Over the years, I tested it in academia, the workplace and the community and I landed in richly rewarding spaces across the world. This entire matter—Rev. Jackson's words, my renewed confidence, my productivity, my achievements all point to the extravagant evidence of God's love for me. Rev. Jackson's words eradicated multiple spoken words about who I am, what I bring to the table, and my destiny. His spoken words propelled affirming words from my parents—especially my mom. My mom thought that I should be a lawyer—civil rights perhaps. She thought that my mind was sharp and my intrigue for details fascinated her. She noticed that the person whom I became through the seasons of my life had lost confidence in myself. She shared with me that I no longer realized how smart I am and she lamented that her daughter now seemed to feel defeated by her lived experiences. Disappointing my parents felt cruel. I had no desire to cause them agony.

Thank God for the turn around. This tribute to the power of words reminds me as a teacher to speak life, confidence, success, hope and peace to my beautiful students. Words often linger in the human heart. I listen to trauma stories and learn that children are traumatized as much by painful words as by violent acts against them. I remain indebted to Rev. Jesse Louis Jackson, Sr., who did not mince words about my mind. He did not need to flatter a little known volunteer who wanted to serve his organization. I, on the other hand, was a wide-eyed, admiring soul who seemed to need to have her say with Rev. Jackson, after every speech that he made. Perhaps I wanted to see if I could match wits with him or ask critical questions. How else would he have known the mental acuity that I possessed? He received my notes. He said that he read them. I felt empowered. Occasionally he would even take the jagged edged, scrappy piece of torn notebook paper with my "brilliant suggestions on it" out of his pocket and show it to me. He was a mentor—kind, gentle and encouraging to this sincere, searching soul.

Because both Rev. Barrow and Dr. Wyatt worked closely with Rev. Jackson, I spent hundreds of hours with them. In their capacity as national leaders in the country, I discovered their influence in Chicago and among other national leaders. I attended church with them, served as their valet, engaged them in lengthy dialogues on topics dear to my heart—the plight of our people, growing tensions between men and women, union activities, and of course the church. These two women: The Rev. Willie Taplin Barrow and Dr. Addie Wyatt had a pulse on the social and political climate in our nation. My close association with them took me into all kinds of meetings and gatherings that otherwise may not have been available to me.

One such meeting was with the initial planning committee members who had gathered to discuss the campaign for the election of Harold Washington as the first black mayor of Chicago, Illinois. What a wow moment for me. All that I knew about Chicago was that Richard Daley ran the city and black people too. The idea that a black man could be elected Mayor of this controversial city with all of its racially charged experiences for any number of Chicago residents awakened in me the need to be present and actively engaged in this venture. Fortunately, Operation PUSH acquainted me with the multiple successful black owned and operated businesses, the successful black entrepreneurs, the gainfully employed black men and women in corporate America, the entertainment industry, sports, education, health, medicine and government. From my perspective, Chicago was a city of two worlds for black people—those who made it and those who were trying to make it. Make it where, you ask? Make it to the summit of their careers or even have a career. Folks in Chicago who needed to either improve or gain skill sets that then allowed them to join the highly qualified and employable candidates in the labor market. I saw far too many people in Chicago who felt stuck in entry level or dead end employment positions.

I was employed by an agency in Chicago that supported the residents in career counseling, job placement, educational opportunities and other activities that could improve the marketability of our clients. Now here we were in multiple gatherings in a variety of venues all discussing the possibility of electing the first black mayor of Chicago. In these different venues, we found inspiration for gathering our wits, putting aside all differences, collecting ourselves through church, civic, fraternal and community organizations that believed in our common goal and vision for Chicago. AsI looked around the space and observed the presence of entertainers, laborers, youth, everyday people as well as "street wise" people, I understood how much we believed in Harold Washington as our candidate. He had many years of experience as an elected official. He exhibited strong legal, people and social skills. He articulated his vision for Chicago and his commitment as an entrusted elected official of our great city. Harold Washington was our idea of the perfect first. Our zeal affected how we thoroughly organized, planned, and with the help of many others in the nation, we successfully elected Harold Washington as the first black mayor of Chicago. I was there front and center, deeply involved and excited about the privilege of my con-nection with these two women—Rev. Barrow and Dr. Wyatt—who were national leaders and how they made this experience possible for me.

Sometime after this positively exhilarating celebration of Harold Washington's victory, a preacher would come to my church: Vernon Park Church of God in Chicago. He would bring a message of hope during a week of revival services. He was the Reverend Dr. Samuel George Hines. He hailed from the island of Jamaica and pastored a church in Washington, DC: Third Street Church of God. He sus-tained a viable social activist connection to Rev. Jackson because of his leadership with Operation PUSH in Washington, DC. I felt an instant affinity for this dear Pastor. In 1970, I met my first Jamaican friend in New York City. Intrigued by this friend's accent, lifestyle, attitude and overall approach to life, I learned to admire the Jamaican people whom I encountered often in my activities in New York. I began to imitate their accent and study their speech patterns. I devel-oped quite an affinity for the Jamaican people. In this way, I had a predisposition to the message of this pastor. Dr. Hines talked about racial reconciliation and forgiveness generally and in South Africa more particularly. I listened intently to his messages each evening and wondered how it could be possible to be reconciled to the gov-ernment of South Africa that then refused to free Nelson Mandela. I participated regularly with the social activists in Chicago who pro-tested the apartheid government in South Africa. I did not hear a message of reconciliation and forgiveness—not even in the church. I heard the message of liberation from oppression, social justice, equity and the absolute dismantling of the government of South Africa. My love for the Jamaican people, because of such fulfilling experiences with them in New York City, and my appreciation for such a revolutionary idea as reconciliation and forgiveness grabbed my attention.

I listened intently to Pastor Hines' account of the biblical mandate for reconciliation and forgiveness and then his practical application of these biblical principles. Pastor Hines' and sociologist John Staggers partnered in the ministry of reconciliation and forgiveness and at the invitation of the Ambassador to South Africa made several trips to South Africa. In a conversation with John Staggers' widow, I learned that their partnership allowed them to function as arbitrators at the table with members of the South African government, members of the African National Congress, Chief Mangosuthu Buthelezi, Chief Minister of KwaZulu, members of the Dutch Reformed Church and others invited to engage in the discussion around South Africa's political future. Their assignments to listen, perhaps functioning as arbitrators, to the multiple voices at the table in South Africa to resolve a centuries long devastating oppression of the Africans by the Afrikaners challenged their spiritual, intellectual and moral sensibilities. The cries and outrage of the peoples of southern Africa had reached the ears of the leadership and the souls of men and women worldwide. With support from compassionate allies across the globe, these men and women demanded the release of Nelson Mandela as well as the dismantling of the apartheid government. Pastor Hines and John Staggers were preaching and teaching racial reconciliation and forgiveness in all forums available to them nationally and internationally.

Pastor Hines in our Chicago revival planted the seeds for this message as he unpacked the biblical foundation for racial reconciliation and forgiveness. The congregation listened curiously. I especially felt both intrigued and compelled by his message. I had been participatory on the militant and protestation side of this issue. My church enjoyed a solid reputation for both social activism and social justice. I tried to wrap my mind around the idea of reconciliation and forgiveness in the context of freedom, liberation from oppression and justice in the land for the abused residents in the cities of South Africa. Pastor Hines advanced the cause for such reconciliation and forgiveness because of how God worked through him and Brother John Staggers, both of whom fully embraced this principle and provided sterling examples in practical living. This all sounded like such a novel idea. So lofty. So unreachable. And yet, I became mesmerized by the possibility of becoming trained by both Pastor Hines and Brother Staggers in the ministry of reconciliation and forgiveness.

To my good fortune, Pastor Hines struggled that week with some vocal issues, a scratchy throat and the threat of laryngitis. As a classically trained vocalist, who had traveled on the road with theatrical ensembles, I learned many health tips for sustaining my voice for all scheduled performances. I assured Pastor Hines that I could share some products from the health food store that would remedy his vocal concerns until he returned to his home in Maryland. He consented to try some of the products. In the parking lot of his accommodations, we engaged in a humorous discussion about each product that I purchased for him. He looked at the labels and ingredients and did not find any of the lozenges or herbs palatable. I assured him that he would see the difference each remaining night of his sermons. During that encounter we laughed about his impatience with allowing some of the throat lozenges to melt in his mouth. He declared that he had no patience for that. I cautioned him that he must be a good patient. That small gesture led to my decision to relocate to Washington, DC to learn from a biblical perspective what Pastor Hines and his other students could teach me about the nature of reconciliation and forgiveness, social justice and liberation.

In my view, racial reconciliation and forgiveness is a life transforming approach to race relations. I could hear the voice of God direct me to give up my need for justice. I knew that Jesus was not a whining wimp! In this way, I knew that giving up my need for justice did not mean to cave into a sense of hopelessness, pathetic loss, or inability to navigate the system of justice in the USA. I learned that giving up my ideas about how justice should be served and now submitting to a biblical perspective would provide me with greater skills going forward. The books of wisdom in the bible and the Psalms provide a vast array of understanding of how God guides his servants to justice. It will not appeal to your five senses or to your cognitive capacity to understand justice as a mere mortal. These biblical principles will rattle your sensibilities, scramble your reasoning abilities, and jar your emotions. If you allow God to speak to your heart through the scriptures and as you wrestle with them through the power of the Holy Spirit's comfort, you will find that you can be used by God to become an instrument of God's peace. God can begin in you the transformation to a person of power that the world could never offer you. This transformation could take you to venues with a message of hope undefined. I know because God, in his perfect love, has done that for the previous life of a radical, angry, militant, woman who began to find violence attractive enough to consider it as an option against oppression, injustice, and unfair practices. My transformed life came as God provided extravagant evidence to me of God's perfect love.

RACE: Riddles, Risks and Rage

Trust in the Lord with all thine heart; and lean not unto thine own understanding. In all thy ways acknowledge him, and he shall direct thy paths. Be not wise in thine own eyes: fear the Lord, and depart from evil. Proverbs 3:5-7 King James Version

God's Perfect Love Melts my Cold Heart

When I was a young girl, I thought that white people faced ONLY one problem: black people. What a riddle. The conundrum revolved around how white people enslaved and "imported" black people to these lands, brutalized, oppressed, dismembered these unsuspecting captives while working them like oxen, camels and hounds. Seemingly, after these slaves picked cotton, built roads, nurtured children, served families and finally experienced liberation from such conditions, white people then behaved as if black people caused all their problems. Fast forward to my youthful naivety in the 1960's, when I was determined to solve the riddle of race relations by examining the Judeo-Christian ethics and biblical principles taught in Sunday School at my Methodist church. Becoming a respectful, morally upright Chrisitan woman guaranteed acceptance among our white Christian brothers and sisters, I thought. Some years later, I embraced Micah 6:8—"He hath shewed thee, O man, what is good; and what doth the LORD require of thee, but to do justly, and to love mercy, and to walk humbly with thy God?" Did not my fellow white Christians recognize that tensions rise and trust dies when we disregard the scriptural teachings? Does Micah inspire us to reach out to others, show compassion to the oppressed, and join in traveling the path that God shows us? I found it so. I tried to appeal to my white Christian friends. They turned away from my face. Sigh.

Could it be that the white Christians neither read nor believed Micah 6:8 in the way that I did? Did God really intend for every follower of Christ to act justly? What if acting justly meant to mind your own business and not be concerned about the demands of civil disobedience and peaceful protests? What did my white Christian brothers and sister understand about loving mercy? Maybe they believed that loving mercy meant to care for those who looked, acted and behaved like they did. Mercy then extends ONLY to themselves and their own families. Now walking humbly before our God perhaps stirred up a race riot evidenced in Tulsa, Oklahoma; Rosewood, Florida; and East St. Louis, Illinois.

I wondered if maybe white Christians believed that walking humbly had only to do with going to their church services, listening to their pastor's teaching and preaching and thereby repeating this same behavior indefinitely—never extending oneself beyond your church, your community, your world! I do not know what the white Christians believed about Micah 6:8; but, I do know how they behaved—not all of them [I did not meet the "good" ones] but too many of them. As a teenager, I always wanted to walk right up the steps and down the aisle into their churches to experience their reaction. Cautioned by the possibility of being injured, I simply never did attend their churches. Too many of our white Christians were silent, absent, and unavailable for support and assistance during the Civil Rights movement that morphed over some decades into the Black Lives Matter movement. One wonders how the power of unity among Christians could have affected quite a different outcome to what we experience today: more lives spared, less blood shed, more light of Christ driving out the darkness of our republic. The riddle continues!

In my integrated high school in the mid-60's, I observed the contemptible behavior of some of our white Christians toward their fellow black students. Regrettably the mass exodus of white students left the black and brown students behind to present themselves as desirable students. In this way, many of our beloved teachers, coaches and staff members behaved toward black and brown students as if we were welcomed to the neighborhood. Around and about San Antonio, I noticed that contempt toward blacks simmered slowly as it met with resistance from local civil rights activists. Socially, politically and economically, our city continued to evolve, finding blacks and browns joining whites to establish greater equity and parity in our city.

I, however, studied race relations on a national level, examining the unfolding of attitudes toward Dr. Martin Luther King, Jr. and the strategies of civil disobedience. Such insights took my thoughts from the riddle to the risk factors of the fight for justice and improved race relations. I wondered why Dr. King and his followers chose to risk their lives fighting for our constitutional rights—enduring such bloody, bruising, battles. As a Christian, I fully embraced the Judeo-Christian ethics and biblical principles pursued by Dr. King and his followers during the Civil Rights movement. I, however, felt challenged by their risks to life and limb to fully gain our constitutional rights. I watched in horror at how our white brothers and sister disregarded their risks and made their civil disobedience experiences as painfully threatening, bloody, bruising, dangerous, horrifying and bitter as possible. I watched in horror and suffered from survivor guilt.

Surprisingly, even though I respected peaceful protests, I entertained the idea of more radical behavior to avenge the injustices. Somehow I thought I must right the wrongs done repeatedly in such blatantly disrespectful, intentional and arrogant behavior. God forbid that I should entertain films where more risky ideas as physical force, bombs and violence used to send an urgent message seemed reasonable. Perish the thought—my parents persisted. We practice non-violent, civil disobedience. We love our enemies. My parents commanded respect because they practiced this behavior. We will forgive. We refuse to hate. We do not bear arms and risk having to use them. We believe that God's word can be realized in this life. I bristled at how I thought such things that made the word of God of little or no effect in my spiritual formation. I suspect anger, revenge, and resistance tried to dominate my thoughts. I meditated on my unacceptable behavior. I realized that I dare not shelve my Christian values. How frightening. Though my Christian upbringing cautioned me to repent, I debated with God: "I am the oppressed, have I not suffered enough? Now, I must repent for a natural response to pain, suffering and brutality toward me and my people?" God won! God's word inspired me to love my neighbor as myself. How difficult and yet necessary because Dr. King taught us that love conquers hate.

Baffled at the absence of white clergy at the marches and demonstrations, I asked my parents, friends, and teachers multiple questions. What could keep Christians from speaking to the images of violence toward peaceful protestors? What could keep Christians from addressing the brutality of those exercising their constitutional rights? How could my fellow Christians disregard the risks taken by peaceful protestors? How could my white Christian brothers and sisters refuse to call to the attention of the nation the desperate pleas for desegregation and the end to racial discrimination? My naivete lingered and my thoughts turned once again to the risks the marchers took for freedom. Haunted by guilt, I wanted to do something meaningful. I yearned to do something!

In the mid-70's I finally joined the peaceful protest movement calling for the end to the apartheid government in South Africa. As a vocalist, I often sang at freedom rallies in Chicago. I aligned with Operation PUSH [People United to Serve Humanity] and supported the other civil rights groups seeking the liberation of the peoples of southern Africa. I felt empowered. I felt purposeful. Both experiences were short lived. The more I participated in the peaceful protests, the more I attended worship services. The more I studied the bible, the more I felt a seething rage welling up within. Why did I sense such rage? Perhaps the cumulative effect of waiting, longing, hoping and working toward justice only to hear the then Ambassador to the United Nations, Andrew Young, share the following words in a speech: "Chicago, Illinois in the 70's was worse than South Africa." What? Living in Chicago during the time of his speech caused me to look around Chicago more earnestly—regrettably, Ambassador Young's words irrefutably established in my mind that our freedom struggle could become endless. We might face countless generations fighting and never knowing such liberation. Justice through peaceful protest, trying to sustain the physical, emotional and spiritual injuries, attempting to brave the risks to life and limb no longer a riddle, now birthing a spirit of rage within my soul. I concluded that my fellow bible reading, bible living white Christians read something in the scriptures that affirmed their silence, compliance, and indifference to my people and our predicament. In this way, I followed a trajectory from riddles to risks to RAGE.

My constrained rage intensified in my matriculation in the university setting. As a junior in college, I enrolled in an African-American literature course. I read W.E.B. DuBois' *Souls of Black Folks* and struggled with the truth found in my own "double consciousness." I read Richard Wright's *Native Son* and struggled with the truth of a black man's plight in the eyes of his white bosses. I read Margaret Walker's works and felt befuddled with the social plight and emotional plague that my people faced. I read, with intense curiosity, the texts of influential and highly esteemed African-American philosophers, sociologists, historians, and scientists. I studied the pathos of Negro spirituals. I listened to them as I once listened to ballads and blues. When I discovered the stories of how the spirituals were used as "runaway to freedom calls" led by Harriet Tubman, I hastened to master the art of delivering these spirituals as a vocalist. I fully understood their pathos and the sound of my voice comforted me. The rage within began to lie dormant. The literature, music and history of the African-American experience in the United States stimulated my thinking. My Fisk University with the most engaging Professor Leslie M. "Doc" Collins inspired my journey and future decisions.

Over the years, I more fully embraced and continued to study the Negro spirituals, examining their origin and the lives of those social activists like Paul Robeson. I received as a gift an album by Paul Robeson, the Renaissance man. I considered him a man for all seasons. He communicated messages of hope through his artistry. His articulation of our course of events and his delivery of the spirituals awakened in me a love for more scholarship in the studies of worldwide liberation movements. I considered myself one, who might advance our cause without risking my life, while managing the brewing rage in my heart.

In 1997, I began to matriculate at Princeton Theological Seminary. Accepted as a member of the Touring Choir, I sang "There Is a Balm in Gilead" and prayerfully delivered in song my hope for a far better future between the "black" and "white" churches. From my perspective, the white churches should have been actively engaged with non-white churches leading the charge for human dignity among all of God's creation. We then should unpack together the scriptures we study, identifying action plans for more effective ways of addressing racial tensions. Princeton Theological Seminary [PTS] provided the foundation for building up my ministry of racial reconciliation and forgiveness. The extraordinary experiences that Princeton provided eased the rage in my soul. During my three year matriculation there I denounced my rage and advanced my commitment to unity. I and a fellow classmate planned a student driven, two-day and four event racial reconciliation and forgiveness experience for the PTS family and broader community. I found God's love at PTS in a totally fulfilling way. I experienced the sweetest victory over all my hateful thoughts, disillusioned notions about white Christians and impatience with justice, mercy and liberation for oppressed people. Prayerfully, I moved from riddles, risks, and rage to reason. I love the scripture that compels us to reason one with another—Isaiah 1:18[a] Come now, and let us reason together, saith the LORD..." What power awaits the one who is willing to come to the table of brother and sisterhood and reason with one another, teasing out issues, principles, ethics, ideas in search of a more desirable way in which to navigate life.

Finally my riddles, risks and rage at the social, political and spiritual circumstances that I and my people faced slammed into a scripture that revolutionized my life: I John 4:16—"And we have known and believed the love that God hath to us. God is love; and he that dwelleth in love dwelleth in God, and God in him."

Over many years of God's extravagant evidence of this aforementioned love for me, I find that I can now BREATHE because I surrendered my need for such human love to the perfect love of God.

I abandoned to God my demanding riddles, my delicate risks and my dangerous rage. I then experienced the balm of God's healing love. I shared the joy of God's refreshing love with others both in and out of this nation. I do not contend bitterly with the harrowing effects of injustice since God's perfect love swept me off my feet. I conquer through a greater resolve and absolute compassion to pursue justice, equity and parity for the oppressed, but not with the seething anger nor the blistering hatred I once held. With God's love in my heart, at the glaring recorded horrors piled high in faces, places, spaces all around our great nation and no longer grieve myself to death. With unrelenting confidence I seek to make a difference in this human race with love and its power to transform and free the souls all the way from earth to heaven. What an unrivaled opportunity.

Princeton Praise

But my God shall supply all your need[s] according to his riches in glory by Christ Jesus. Philippians 4:19—King James Version

I drove through the imposing yet welcoming iron gates of Princeton Theological Seminary gawking at the meticulously manicured grounds. Unimaginable for me the very idea of matriculating at this Flagship seminary internationally known for its scholarship, academic excellence and stellar place of preparation for ministry. I gazed upon the beautifully manicured grounds anticipating the privilege of roaming to and fro across the campus expanse. My excitement intensified now recalling my first visit to the campus in March 1997. Princeton Theological Seminary required from me cognition that I needed to test. Can I keep up with these academically gifted students some twenty-five years my junior? How would my eyes, brain, and ears support me during this time of academic rigor for a three year period before the completion of 90 hours required for the Master of Divinity degree? The class of 2000 found itself with Rhodes Scholars, Phi Beta Kappa graduates, Dean's lists graduates, attorneys, and a wholesome list of others from lucrative corporate positions. Why had they left their positions to come to seminary?

The Back Story

From my perspective, I only left to attend seminary, a demanding teaching career that once smelled of roses and then began to smell of rotting eggs. My final teaching year in the District of Columbia Public Schools after a gorgeous nine years spiraled downward into the abyss of an egregious political act against me because of a racially inflamed incident regarding the teaching of Advanced Placement courses to predominantly white students. Such an incident marred by once glowing years in the nation's capital school system. I grew more than weary from the legal proceedings to address the replacement of my position by a white male who argued that as a paraprofessional in my department, he noted my incompetencies for teaching the Advanced Placement course. He maneuvered his way politically into a teaching position with this course.

Apparently he and perhaps a few other colleagues convinced students that he could prepare them more adequately than I for the Advanced Placement exam. This dear soul, I had been told, never even appropriately followed the system's guidelines for becoming a classroom teacher. I felt betrayed by the system, abandoned by my school administration, and humiliated by my students and colleagues. I, however, discovered that my issue now added to a longer list of issues in this esteemed and well known high school in DC's west of the park community. Fortunately, I felt greatly encouraged by my teacher's union representative. She expressed her disgust for the way in which the system and my administration handled the entire matter of a paraprofessional being permitted to "take over" my classroom instructional tasks without any due process for me. I had never even received an average evaluation. I collected and reviewed my nearly dozen teacher evaluations and discovered that they were all above average. Regrettably, all of my preparation, earnest desire to improve skills, and long-suffering with the tensions in our English department did not render me a suitable candidate to teach the predominantly white students in our Advanced Placement English classes.

My union representative advised me that she deemed it necessary to invite a group of Georgetown law students to review my case and share their findings regarding a racially charged and inflamed matter that clearly violated the teacher of record's civil rights. My professional journey, now acutely disturbed by the smell of incompetence that did not have a paper trail or verbal confirmation by any stretch of the imagination. I could have followed the legal opportunity to address the egregious nature of this offense, but chose instead to follow the leading of my Creator, Redeemer, and Sustainer of life–take the offer to matriculate at Princeton Theological Seminary, pursue the Master of Divinity degree and find God's purpose for my season there.

Little did I know to what extent God would choose to use--as a balm in Gilead—the harrowing effects of the emotional and spiritual trauma caused by the abrupt ending to my teaching assignment at Woodrow Wilson High School. Clearly, my departure remained a buzz of discussion among colleagues and students evidenced--a few months later–by a mean-spirited, maligning and character assassinating article in the school newspaper. How could I have severed my relationship with DC Public Schools under the cloud of incompetence when I had won some ten awards and grants for further study including a major award to attend Oxford University. I reviewed all of the steps that I took to remain both competent and effective with my students. I satisfied none of my accusers who enjoyed privilege in their wealthy neighborhoods in DC's Ward 3. They never gave me an audience. I reached out in multiple ways to get an understanding. Sigh! I developed a healthy rapport with a number of the students–all to no avail.

I received the news from colleagues that my southern roots, blackness, and matriculation at one of those "small black colleges" labeled me as suspect for mediocrity. Unimaginable, the steps that I took to demonstrate that I could perform as competently as my fellow Advanced Placement English teachers, all of whom were white. I, in a manner of speaking, knocked myself out to present myself as equally intelligent as my white colleagues. One day I could hear clearly the voice of God: "This is the last time in your life that you will seek to prove to white people that you are their equal. You will never, ever do this again." The issue for me stemmed from years of a Jim Crow lifestyle in the southern and southwest regions of the country. The behavior toward me regarding this teaching assignment triggered a review of multiple disadvantages, indignities, insecurities and indecencies my foreparents and I experienced in an incredible effort to demonstrate ourselves worthy of serious consideration for opportunities normally unavailable to us. Such experiences at Wilson in the English department, reminiscent of unsettling experiences with race, affected my sense of well being. Indeed I attended a "small black college" in the south. Actually, I attended a renowned university in Nashville, Tennessee with an outstanding record of high achieving blacks who offered greatness to the nation in a wide variety of government, community, business and professional venues. I attended the celebrated home of the Jubilee Singers–Fisk University. My white colleagues misrepresented my esteemed university as a "small black college in the south!" I, however, know without question that my fellow classmates at Fisk University could compete with the best students anywhere in our world. They were well traveled, mentally competent, and fully capable of contributing to the resources, achievements and performances that this human experience offered. I struggled to believe in myself because of the prevailing rejection by the society at large and the incident of my socio-economic inferiority while matriculating at Fisk. Nonetheless, I appreciated the incredible joy of sharing with some of America's brightest minds during my all too brief two years at Fisk.

Alas, nothing about my character, my academic preparation, my professional journey or my years of receiving study grants and awards from the National Endowment for the Humanities served the purposes of my entitled by virtue of whiteness fellow accusers. God bless these dear souls. After unending dialogues with many of these white colleagues over my tenure in DC Public Schools, it seems as if they believe that black and mediocrity were synonymous. These dear colleagues thereby determined that black teachers should NOT teach their children. Apparently in the minds of these colleagues who spoke freely—"small black colleges in the south" and incompetence—marked the height to which blacks achieved–perhaps more particularly in the field of education. Black teachers providing instruction in the *elite* College Board's Advanced Placement program were incongruous mixtures.

Finally, I looked to God for healing, deliverance and restoration. In this way, Princeton Theological Seminary [PTS] appropriately stimulated my battered mind, soothed my wounded spirit, calmed my frazzled emotions, quieted the shouts of condemnation and ignited my confidence in the absolute decency of the human family. From my perspective, I desperately needed to restore my good name. I wanted to relate to God and watch God's hand upon my life in a different view—even whiter, if you will, than the Wilson High School, DC Ward 3 community. I deeply longed to find a place of rest for my weary soul and Princeton entirely fulfilled all of afore-mentioned needs. I confess, I felt intimidated by the demographics of our class. I felt more uncertain than ever before about my cognitive capabilities. I recalled the twelve + years that I spent with the College Board's Advancement Placement program and the sustained effort I made to demonstrate my competence among my colleagues. Now, here I stand in an even more demanding academic environment after having been knocked out of the ring in my high school setting and what could I expect of my mental acuity? Suddenly, I remembered the words, shared with me in 1979, spoken by the Reverend Jesse Louis Jackson, Sr, President of Operation People United to Serve Humanity [PUSH] and the Rainbow Coalition. I received the following words through a message from Rev. Jackson's Press Secretary's special friend: "Carol has a razor sharp mind." I rehearsed those words repeatedly, and embraced them to such an extent that finally I developed enough confidence to pursue other personal and professional dreams. I focused upon just how I could support and offer to the PTS Class of 2000 something memorable and of significance.

Among my course work obligations, additionally, I received the privilege of membership in the Princeton Touring Choir. I cannot begin to describe how I experienced such a richly rewarding three years in this choir. Opportunities to sing solos amazed me. Because I was the age of many of the students' parents, I considered myself to be the honorary "Mom"of our choir. I, however, found myself behaving with my classmates more like a peer to them. I thoroughly enjoyed all of our conversations regarding the demanding syllabi that we faced in our coursework. I loved talking about music with them because they possessed excellent sight reading skills and shared them freely with me. Our choir director showered kindness upon his choir members in ways that brought out beautiful music. He spoke softly and behaved graciously toward us with his inimitable style. I loved to sing for and with Dr. Martin Tel. He believed in all of his choir members and inspired them to reach down in their souls for the profound sense of the composer's desire while singing his or her music. On every occasion, Martin inspired joyful singing. Prayerfully, we ministered to the awaiting ears in every congregation and audience where we sang. What a gift from God to be a member of the Princeton Touring Choir, the PTS Chapel choir and the PTS Cathedral choir. I felt elated to sing the diverse pieces of music offered each rehearsal.

At PTS, I witnessed extravagant evidence of God's perfect love for my life. Regrettably, I exercised a poor judgment call in befriending a younger male classmate, who was a year ahead of me. He eventually expressed contempt for me. Sigh. This encounter reminded me of how I needed ONLY to accept God's perfect love and leave my desire for romantic love, marriage and the family at the altar and never pick it up again. I did not use good judgment in befriending this dear younger male student. As a result, I put myself in a precarious position that could have misrepresented my character. By God's grace, both I and the younger male student worked through our communication conflict. Prayerfully, some twenty-one years later, we are no longer rehearsing that bittersweet, troubled encounter that went quite wrong. In my heart, I knew that I only wanted to be friends in the most wholesome sense. I never meant to communicate anything deceptive. How could things spiral so quickly out of control? By God's grace, this classmate and I are better for our encounter.

No matter how often or how much my classmates celebrated my music ministry and my friendships across the landscape of the seminary, I still wrestled with insecurities. Could it be that I had taken such a beating in DC Public Schools during my final year at Woodrow Wilson Senior High School in Ward 3 that I wore that experience like a scarlet letter? Suffice to say that the incident of brutality toward my psyche and my professional performance exasperated me. How could a good God allow such a professional bludgeoning among colleagues whom I loved; among students whom I cherished; among families whom I respected. What went wrong that humiliation was my signature before I left DC Public Schools.

By contrast, just three years later, honor and celebration characterized my signature when I graduated from Princeton Theological Seminary. For every injury and insult in DC Public Schools, God provided applause, accolades and affirmation at Princeton Theological Seminary. I cannot tell you the whole story–though I wish I could. It is a story of redemption and reconciliation. For every insult by a white brother or sister in DC Public Schools, PTS provided a pardon. I could be a poster girl for Princeton Theological Seminary–forever etched in my soul is their hallmark of compassion for a weary traveler.

Nonetheless, regrouping and gearing up to compete with these privileged students at Princeton Theological Seminary now took all of my mental, emotional and spiritual energies. Because I was the age of most of their parents, a vocalist, a member of the touring choir, and a very personable classmate, I made friends easily. My classmates thought it strange that I would live in the dorm instead of the campus housing some 2.5 miles away that offered independent apartments. Humph, I did not want to be in any way disconnected from seminary life. Though I was 50 years old, I thought of myself as a late bloomer–maybe more so—a cloaked 30 year old. Laughably, the students did not see me that way. Never mind, I stayed in the dorm my entire three years. I ate in the dining hall, worked as a banquet server and fully embraced every aspect of seminary life as if I were the median seminary student age of 25. I fiercely loved my time there and appreciated the way in which God opened the Princeton door. I had so much to prove to myself.

Remarkably, I had voice lessons the entire three years during my tenure as a member of the touring choir. One of my professors declared that I had sung my way through the seminary. I really needed to see what kind of brain power I possessed. Princeton showed me. I struggled to no end attempting to manage the volume of reading assignments. My writing never quite made the mark of an A. The B assigned to my essays troubled me. Sometimes, the theological discussions baffled me. Occasionally, the Old and New Testament lectures eluded me. What was my problem? All of my concerns were addressed when I heard the highly esteemed Professor Bruce Manning Metzger share the following paraphrased statements:

Professor Metzger offered these words in a guest lecturer venue: Perhaps you realize that you are studying the Holy Bible in three ways:

1. For devotional purposes
2. For research and writing purposes [scholarship]
3. For sermon preparation and teaching purposes

After Dr. Metzger shared more extensively on the above principles, I no longer felt lost and incapable of asking a meaningful question in either the Old or New Testament classes.

Let me brag a little about Princeton Theological Seminary. First of all, the seminary in those years before 9/11 in the USA proudly held a respectable endowment and offered many students scholarships. Such scholarships allowed the seminary to attract the best and the brightest students. Our faith at PTS is from a Calvinist theological perspective. Nonetheless, students from all other religious persuasions were welcomed and contributed to the life of our seminary studies.

I sometimes found myself struggling with the academics and excelling with the music, the campus life and winning new friends. I realized that I loved the people more than the principles we studied. I engaged colleagues all the time. I listened attentively to their stories and celebrated their joys. I empathize with their struggles and prayed for their difficulties. Surely I could master some of the academic study as well. And I did. Alas, I chose to specialize in ethics. Why did I choose ethics? Primarily because of my keen interest in reconciliation and forgiveness. I, however, soon discovered that my scholarship skills continued to bow to my people skills. I was a creative thinker more than a linear thinker. Accused of hyperbole, I often seemed to encounter professorial fatigue. Accordingly, I wondered if I should become a social worker rather than a pastor. Because of the scholarship demands, I wondered if I were out of my lane in ethics. Perhaps I should have chosen the music and worship department in which I could more easily specialize and advance the scholarship there. Here I could have done both spoken word and vocals with theological underpinnings from the perspective of African-American spirituals and gospel music. I chose ethics to challenge myself. I nearly missed the opportunity to graduate because of the harsh reality of a thesis that challenged me to the marrow of my being. Alas, I burned hundreds of relaxation candles to complete this thesis even when my stomach demanded that I rest from my anxiety over this research project–a thesis in which I wondered what in the world I was trying to say. My compassionate professor responded to my thesis with most helpful comments, accepted my research and signed off on my final project for graduation purposes. Whew!

Following those final days of stretching my brain to articulate some credible ideas in my thesis, I relaxed a bit and began to think about life after our graduation ceremony and related activities. Then, the most incredible gift dropped into my lap for the asking. This is the story:

A Gift from God

Following our Baccalaureate service, two of my colleagues and I began to muse about our seminary experience and our plans following graduation. We talked about summer fun after three demanding years of study at PTS. The curriculum and syllabi left no student without clear notice that PTS wanted its graduates to endure academic rigor, ministerial effectiveness, and personal application of the scriptures in their chosen careers before awarding them a degree. We laughed. We sighed. We remembered. We reminisced.

Suddenly I had a confession to make: "My sisters, I said, I have a very selfish prayer request. When we pray, will you pray with me for this admittedly selfish request." I shared with them that I wanted, as a graduate gift from God, to go on the Reformation journey with the Nassau Presbyterian Church. I was made aware of the months of detailed preparation for this journey, the weeks of intense bible study, and the overall plans for a delightful pilgrimage following the paths of Calvin and Luther in Europe. It was a dream trip. It could be either 10 days or 17 days in duration. It cost several thousand dollars. My Mom had given each of her four children a monetary gift to save for "rainy day" expenses. I thought that I would use that gift and, if necessary, supplement costs with my credit card.

I, however, wanted God to give me this trip in this way. I wanted some dear soul who would make the trip to realize that the trip was overly ambitious. I wanted him or her to then decide that he or she would gift the trip to a Nassau church member or seminary graduate. I wanted it to then be the 17 day trip instead of the 10 day trip. I wanted all of this to work out in just a few hours of the next morning so that I could prepare accordingly. I knew that it was selfish of me to want someone else to forfeit their trip so that I could have it, but I also knew that I was telling God the honest truth and maybe I could just get on board with this trip at the 9th hour and pay for it myself.

We prayed. We bid one another farewell and two of us went on with graduation plans, while our second year sister friend went on her way with her summer plans. Through the night, I repented for my selfish request. It was quite late, something like 2:30 am when I finally began to feel sleepy. I decided to test my faith in God. I would not set the alarm. I asked God to awaken me and let me make the call to the church at no later than 9:03 am. I knew the Director of Christian Education would arrive on time to her office and I wanted to catch her within the first five minutes to see if I could talk her into adding me to the guest list for this trip. Unbelievably, God awakened me out of a deep sleep at 9:00am. I shook myself for a moment and then called Nassau Presbyterian Church at 9:03 am. I asked for Nancy, the trip director, by name because I had met her before. She had just walked in the door and was a few feet from her office door when the receptionist alerted her to my phone call. She picked up my call and listened as I made the case for my desire to be added to her guest list. She laughed–seemingly quite surprised at my rather unusual request. After all, the group was leaving in just a few days. Though she laughed that kind of laugh that tells you that she does not suffer foolishness, she remained quite gracious in explaining to me that if anything changed, she would add me to the tour guest list.

I then laughed because I knew that I could not be added to the guest list at this point considering that this trip had been in the works for over a year and intensively for many months. I told her that I probably should not even ask her to consider me if someone dropped out because I would be using a portion of money set aside for emergencies to pay for this trip. She laughed and said: "Anything is possible. If something changes, I will let you know!"

She then said a kind farewell to me and I sat on the side of my bed and smiled. No trip for me. Suddenly my telephone rang. It was Nancy and she was quite out of character. Her shock and enthusiasm resounded throughout her voice now some decibels above her normal tone. She said: "CarolAnn, CarolAnn, the most amazing thing just happened. While you and I were on the telephone, another call came into the front office. The Office Manager took the call. The guest said: "Tell Nancy that in hindsight, this trip is overly ambitious for me. I have decided, though I have 100% insurance, to not only gift it, but to gift it to either a Nassau member or seminary student. Let her know that she can do this straightaway." Nancy then said that since I had just spoken to me. She would give the trip to me. She then said that it was my good fortune to catch her because she was going directly into a meeting at 9:05 am. Once again, a preposterous story for others and extravagant evidence for me of God's perfect love. God's perfect love even in the absence of–my deepest longing–a loving husband, children and a nuclear family with whom to share this testimony. I shared it with my colleagues, perhaps many of whom found it to be an exaggerated tale. Every word of this story is TRUE.

I prepared for the trip, went along with the group and had the most fulfilling time of my life. What a joy. What a privilege. What a great God. Following the path of John Calvin and Martin Luther, we both received lectures and visited cities in Switzerland, Germany, Belgium, and France. In my excitement, I could have turned backwards somersaults in iron chains. Wow, the mystery and magic of this educational, cultural, and spiritual journey–placing our feet on the paths of these church fathers.

In my quiet hour, I simply reflected upon the extravagant evidence in my life of God's love. The circumstances of this trip represented a fairy tale for some but an encounter with the power and authority of God to be specific in God's answer when I was specific in my petition. In this way, God continues to show his great love for me. Though I would have rejoiced to have had a travel companion for the trip, I settled myself in the company of the group members–experiencing first one adventure and then another with different members of the group. We got along beautifully and took full advantage of this most unusual and one-time journey to retrace the paths of Calvin and Luther.

God's perfect love and his extravagant evidence sent me out from Princeton Theological Seminary with two monetary awards at graduation, a position of honor in the Baccalaureate Service, and a graduation gift that God alone provided to me. Periodically, I forfeited sweet peace, feeling anxious among these terribly bright students and brilliant scholars. God showed me a special assignment during my final months at the seminary. I carried it out with the overwhelming support of my classmate, Case Thorpe. He and I made seminary history with our four-event, student driven reconciliation and forgiveness seminar. What unspeakable Jesus joy I took with me in May 2000 as I exited the proud and powerfully imposing iron gates of my beloved Princeton Theological Seminary.

Kind Keisha

Delight thyself also in the LORD; And he shall give thee the
desires of thine heart. Psalm 37:4—King James Version

What a privilege to meet this kind young lady whose outward beauty, exceeded only by her inward beauty, afforded her the opportunity–should she accept it–for product modeling. Keisha did not seem to recognize how God gifted her with such a pretty face. She is the first born and only daughter of a military dad and a mom who worked as an office administrator. Her parents are church members with me. She and her only brother lived with their parents in Columbia, Maryland. Fortunately for me, the family lived only a few blocks away from my home. How convenient. Access to each other for all kinds of transportation needs worked simply beautifully. Transporting one another around and about our church and civic activities kept us feeling secure and safe during the late evening hours. We occasionally walked to one another's houses. Keisha and I love movies, concerts, revivals, cooking shows, creative and entrepreneurial endeavors. As often as possible, Keisha and I journeyed around and about to areas that helped us determine how to launch our entrepreneurial vision–we designed travel accessories using ecologically friendly fabrics. We thought that the use of plastic bags could be substantially reduced if travelers would consider our eco-friendly, fabric travel products–shoe bags, laundry bags, jewelry bags and what not pouches. We customized our products according to some six to eight different fabric designs and three different sizes for the shoe and laundry bags. We designed baby bibs but put that plan aside because of the possibility of issues related to fabric allergies for infants. We kept our templates.

Over a few months, Keisha and I established an aunt:niece relationship. We fashioned ourselves as aspiring entrepreneurs and with limited budgets, we knocked on a few doors to seek financial support and manufacturing assistance. Our entrepreneurial activities took many daytime and evening hours over a number of months, but we left room to explore documentaries at the theater, cultural events, nutrition books and outdoor fun. In January 2015, Keisha and I viewed the Joy Mangano movie titled, *Joy.* Both of us became so inspired by Joy's story that we took the leap of faith to pursue two distinctly different projects. One project established my 501c3 ministry about which Keisha and I were excited. The other project, *Des and Deb's Designs,* established our profit making travel products.

We worked to identify persons of interest who would serve as board members for the 501c3 *All is Well Ministries, Inc.* non-profit. We successfully signed on six different members of the board. Since that time, one member has passed away, another is battling stage 4 cancer, and two others have relocated to different states in the nation. I wrote several bible studies and housed them in my curriculums for Christian education with *All is Well Ministries, Inc.* Keisha and I designed and constructed the travel products with the hope of launching in the major markets our brand–*Des and Deb Designs*– named in memory of my mom, Odessa, and in honor of my youngest sister, Debbie. Both my mom and my sister inspired my sense of fashion and interior design. Keisha and I have placed these two modest efforts on hold at the moment. We expect that someday these ideas may revolve into concrete products that generate income for advancing the kingdom of God. This, I believe. I refuse to abandon this hope. I resist the temptation to give in, give up, or give out. I believe in the mission of *All is Well Ministries, Inc.* and the unlimited manufacturing possibilities of *Des and Deb's Designs.* For now, I shall await God's extravagant evidence and action!

After the summer of 2015, Keisha and I found a few more summers to roam about with our vision for ministry and entrepreneurship. We attended concerts, church activities, journeyed to Wilmington, North Carolina, Mount Vernon, New York, and made frequent fun-filled quick trips to York, Pennsylvania. Keisha loved

York. There she found a lovely lakeview area where she pondered and enjoyed the landscape, sunsets, and fishermen. I loved the spot as well. In the area of York, where we visited, we found story book houses with gardens and trellises that attracted our attention. We imagined these houses, owned by us and then rented to friends for summer getaways. We imagined bringing children from the inner cities to these peaceful surroundings and allowing them to fish, hike, bicycle, jog and roam about the pretty little areas that we discovered.

Keisha patiently worked with me and supported all of my creative endeavors. She assisted me as much as possible with the launch of both the ministry and the travel products. These days, she and I both find ourselves in San Antonio, Texas after my unexpected return from Hungary because of COVID 19 and her desire to gain new footing in a brand new city. Here in San Antonio, we continue to pursue our dreams. We must be patient with the on-going reports of the global pandemic and its aftermath. We must protect our health and trust that someday we will have a less threatening health crisis in our world.

I continue to smile as I reflect upon the number of occasions when I encouraged Keisha to spend quality time with her peers. I am quite her senior. Her quick response brought such joy to my soul: "I'm good. I'm where I want to be, hanging out with my adventurous Aunt CarolAnn." She advised me that she often had to decompress because of my energies. She shared that she sometimes returned home from a long day's summer outing with me and needed to roll out the energy that I transferred to her. I laughed uncontrollably at how my imagination conjured up caricatures of Keisha decompressing from my energy–hilarious!

Keisha and I galavanted about the Washington, DC, northern Virginia and Maryland suburban areas seeing, knowing and being sister friends who were on a mission. We simply enjoyed tons of fun exploring sites and venues where we learned new ideas and met engaging personalities. We laughed, cried, worked and prayed together to the most incredible satisfaction of my very soul. Like a gardener's delightful moment after seeding, cultivating, nurturing his gardens and then realizing a harvest of nature's bounty in florals and vegetation, I invested in the spiritual, emotional, and mental development of my dear Keisha and watched her blossom into a confident and productive young woman on the move. My heart tried to say thank you to God who loved me so much that he would fulfill a desire for a daughter figure in my heart by bringing Keisha across my path. Keisha fulfilled my dreams for a loving spiritual niece with whom I could do life. She remains dear to me because of our unnumbered memory making adventures during my concluding six years of life on the east coast of the USA.

The Back Story

I returned to the USA from Chiang Mai, Thailand in May 2017. Again, I did not want to return home so soon. When I serve on the mission field, I feel like a giant–like an eagle soaring high above the earth. Soaring with such a strong sense of direction, purpose and fulfillment. Sometimes when I return home from the mission field, I feel less like an eagle and more like a canary. I sense that I am caged and flitting about in a not large enough space; and, I am singing for my supper, chirping to entertain myself, longing for the opened cage door so that I can be free again. I wish that I didn't feel that way. I confess, it has happened to me five times since I first experienced the joy of my international field experience in 1999 as a seminary student. In my internship there in Fortaleza, Ciara, Brazil, I established myself as a fellow seminary student with my colleagues in our dorm. I learned enough Portuguese combined with my little Spanish language skills and I forged a most fulfilling relationship with my colleagues. My advisor shared with me that the farewell program indicated to him how much my colleagues appreciated their time with me. We enjoyed the most meaningful send off. They roasted me and each comment extended my life. I wanted so much to do more to be a blessing to my Brazilian colleagues. They warmed my heart at every level of engagement. What a privilege to have loved them dearly. I suffer from separation anxiety and I always want to return to the former places I have known. I learned to accept that I cannot always return but I can carry such invigorating memories in my spirit. I loved my time with my fellow seminarians. Each new day brought an exotic adventure.

Nonetheless, I returned this time from Thailand. I loved the joy of reuniting with many friends, my church family, and more adventures in Columbia, Maryland. I especially loved returning to my road runner, Keisha, who met me at the airport upon my landing at the Thurgood Marshall Baltimore Washington International airport. She seemed as joyful as ever to receive her Aunt CarolAnn. She laughed at how I was ready to go to one of our favorite eateries. She thought that I should be plenty tired and travel weary. We laughed and off we went to our first of many adventures.

A couple of days later, Keisha and I discussed my return to my former sewing teacher Mayda [name changed to protect her privacy]. When I contacted Mayda she advised me that she was having her home renovated and would no longer teach private students. Though I felt quite disappointed to lose her as my teacher, I trusted God that someone else at JoAnn's Fabrics might consent to tutor me. Actually, I felt such a loss as I had to accept Mayda's decision. Somehow the words "here I go again" and the sense of another misstep crept upon me. I realized many years past that streams of income provide the opportunity to sustain your general budget and allow for discretionary funds for supporting–free of credit card debt–a number of charitable organizations, entrepreneurial endeavors, personal gift giving and family vacations. In the absence of streams of income, those of us in the helping professions simply do not earn a sufficient enough income to spread the wealth. I watched my sister give her life as a Social Worker seeking to find homes for both foster and adopted children. She worked over 8 hours a day most of the time. She never earned the kind of money that her work ethic, credentials and commitment deserved. Such would be the case with my career as a teacher. I usually stayed at school three hours past the end of the school day seeking methods, lesson plans, materials and other ways to inspire my students' toward academic excellence.

Well, here we were again. Keisha and I are trying to find the path to entrepreneurial success. We accepted that Mayda may not be tied to my entrepreneurial destiny. After processing the matter, we focused upon going forward. Keisha and I did find a new teacher–Beth Ann [name changed to protect her privacy]. This dear soul abounded in teaching energy. I enjoyed several sewing classes with Beth Ann. She and I bonded and explored some time together as we pursued sewing useful products. We assessed the designs and construction necessary for attractive eco-friendly, fabric travel accessories. We socialized as we swapped war stories about our personal and professional journeys.

When Keisha and I put our heads together to discover Plan B, we thought that Beth Ann would like to join us as a partner in an entrepreneurial effort. Keisha and I found the products we would pursue. We searched for the fabrics that would be suitable for our travel accessories. Beth Ann helped me to take everything that I created to the next level. Possessing excellent sewing and design skills, Beth Ann taught me how to prepare additional products for my venture. Beth Ann, Keisha and I became a trio–though too short-lived. We searched for natural fabrics and found ourselves examining accessories to distinguish our brand of travel products. I kept telling Beth Ann that she, Keisha and I could become a team of adventure seeking entrepreneurs. We could design ecologically friendly fabrics into functional travel accessories: shoe covers, laundry bags, make-up kits, and jewelry pouches. Such accessories would protect our nation from the use of plastic bags and their unfriendly composition to all of the waterways.

I even began to attend classes at Howard Community College [HCC] as a student in their entrepreneurial program. Convinced that with the appropriate skills, I could make something of my business, I took several courses at HCC. Just as I thought "Ureka," more turbulence headed my way. This storm brought Tsunami winds and waters for my business ventures. I lost my home to a Short Sale. Earlier with my first entrepreneurial endeavor, I designed door covers that prevented wind/air drafts at the doors of homeowners. After a horrific debacle with the wrong size of the original 450 plus shipment of the door covers, the products arrived from China to the east coast–but not in my home state of Maryland. Now I had to have the bulky items shipped from the port in New Jersey to a suitable warehouse in the immediate area of my home in Howard County. I felt overwhelmed with the details of securing the products in a neighboring warehouse that then must be transported to a storage center for long term safe keeping. Because the size of the door covers were not from the original sample from China and were not the size of the standard American door, I now had to seek an alternative use for them. After several months, I decided that the entire experience resulted in my need to do three things:

a) Protect my health from this terrific loss of income due to the debacle of a product that arrived other than the original sample size;

b) Find suitable homes for the products and trust that they would be useful;

c) Endure this extraordinary teaching moment and know that I must not allow it to ruin my life.

"What kind of misstep could be worse than this one?" I thought. What a great financial, emotional, and professional loss. Thank God I sustained my sanity at the conclusion of that long road traveled that resulted in a frustrating, failed effort.

With this business loss, then some time after that the loss of my home, combined with the gifting of my worldly possessions, punctuated by the inability to make my travel products move swiftly to a manufacturer and to daily earnings, I felt defeated by yet another misstep in securing my finances. My only consolation came when I realized that a number of my personal friends and neighbors lost their homes as well during such a downturn of the economy. Here we all were making critical adjustments in our lifestyles. I wondered if some of my friends were dreamers too. I noticed that several of my friends and I had invested in entrepreneurial endeavors that dissipated. With my door covers, I did extensive research, prepared a substantial business plan, checked in with engineers regarding my product's feasibility, prayed for many months and even contracted with a patent lawyer—all to an undesirable ending when the original product sample was perfectly sized to the standard American door, but the shipped products were inches off for reasons I will never understand. How the disconnect between the sample product and the shipped products occurred remains a mystery as of the writing of this book.

Keisha faithfully committed to assisting me through the devastation of all my losses. She assisted me with the donations to charitable organizations of most of my earthly goods. As a senior citizen with several Master's degrees, energy, good health, ideas, and an unrivaled work ethic, I could not understand why failure chased me like the hungry lion chased the wilderbeast. So, where was God's perfect love in this instance? To tell you the truth, God's perfect love landed me right where I needed to be. More extravagant evidence of God's perfect love came with a sudden phone call from Maria Elgut, who through a series of unexpected events, assisted me in my God ordained trip to Hungary in Eastern Europe.

You will read about this miracle in the chapter titled *Hungary Heals*. What a fitting title for an experience that extended my life by years. Tensions relieved, heartache soothed, energies renewed, love restored, joy refreshed, skills strengthened and more in the blessed nation of Hungary. How I long to return to a sweet little village named Torokszentmiklos. How I long to see the faces again of my students, my colleagues at my beautiful school and my neighbors on Almasy Street. In Hungary, in the countryside, I discovered a whole new world of love, friendship, acceptance and affirmation as an English teacher. I loved the children, the staff, the community and my new life in Hungary. God's perfect love, once more demonstrated in extravagant evidence, because my experience in Hungary was anything but ordinary, hum drum and blase. It was beautiful, brilliant and a blessing. Though unexpectedly interrupted by COVID-19, even in that I found peace. I then begin to use the time to write my transformation story. I confess, some days, I thought I wanted to float into the stratosphere from Hungary. I thoroughly enjoyed my experience even with the minimal hiccups.

Keisha has quite a fascination with the culture, food and films of South Korea. In this way, she and I want to visit South Korea sooner rather than later; and perhaps sometime, we can even share time with Sue Polgar in my beloved village of Torokszentmiklos, Hungary. Keisha represents the extravagant evidence of yet another instance of God's perfect love in my life. I thank God for Keisha.

Missionary Miracles

*And Jesus answered and said, Verily I say unto you, There is
no man that hath left house, or brethren, or sisters, or father,
or mother, or wife, or children, or lands, for my sake, and the
gospel's but he shall receive an hundredfold now in this time,
houses, and brethren, and sisters, and mothers, and children,
and lands, with persecutions; and in the world to come eternal
life. But many that are first shall be last; and the last first.*
Mark 10:29-31 [King James Version]

Kathi Sellers passed away recently. She and her husband, Pastor
Wayne Sellers, served as missionaries in Latin America. When I
connected with Kathi, she was a staff member of Global Strategy,
Church of God Ministries, Inc., Anderson, Indiana. As I celebrate
the fingerprint that she left upon my life, I thought sharing our story
would bring me comfort. I continue to wrestle with the loss of this
devoted missionary/administrator who initiated—in colloquial terms,
she jump start—my missionary service life.

The Back Story

While Reverend Suzanne Haley was consulting at the Church
of God [CHOG] headquarters in Anderson, Indiana on a leadership
development initiative and commuting from Maryland to Indiana
monthly, she arranged for me to meet Kathi Sellers. During Suzanne's
days as Associate Pastor at Long Reach Church of God (Columbia,
Maryland) she explored with me my interest in vocational ministry,
which even then, included global missions. Since I graduated from

Princeton Theological Seminary [PTS] in 2000 at fifty-three years of age, I sometimes thought of myself as a late bloomer and I needed to move through life more expeditiously. Nonetheless, I learned in 1985 to persevere and never again abandon my professional dreams or ministry vision. In this way, some twelve years after graduation (now 2012), I yearned for opportunities in full time ministry that matched my skills and credentials. I, therefore, listened attentively as Kathi Sellers and I engaged in lengthy conversations regarding my preparation for and interest in the mission field.

Inasmuch as I am a certified English teacher, I rehearsed the fact that I qualify to teach English across the world. If I knew anything, surely I would know how to teach English language skills. I reflected upon what I learned through multiple National Endowment for the Humanities grants, as well as a Morris and Gwendolyn Cafritz grant to study in Oxford, England. I contemplated how I actively sought after and participated in teacher's workshops across the District of Columbia. Intrigued by the possibility of incorporating technology, I reviewed the lesson plans I created for my English classes. I examined the curriculum I created using my music and arts training to engage this current generation. I analyzed best practices from my years of working both with the National Council of Teachers of English as well as Educational Testing Service and the College Board. I felt prepared. I maintained a teachable spirit. My Princeton matriculation enhanced all of my English writing skills. My Master of Divinity degree from PTS represented knowledge and ministry preparation and, over a three year period, I completed ninety hours of coursework in theology, ethics, speech, worship, choral music, old and new testament and church history. As a member of the Princeton Touring Choir all three years there, I continued my vocal training and preparedness for music ministry. How encouraging to sing in a seminary community that embraced my vocal gifts and actually invited me to sing for every aspect of the seminary's life. Because I studied the principles of the ministry of reconciliation and forgiveness under the tutelage of Dr. Samuel George Hines, I joined and actively participated in two campus organizations theologically unlike one another. I forged healthy relationships with my classmates who reminded me that I was their parents' age. I sang, smiled, studied, and shared in campus wide activities with my fellow students, sometimes laughing as I remembered that I was twice their age. I thought of myself as an "extreme makeover 25 year old!" I learned and I earned my degree. Again, I rehearsed all these things in my mind believing that this missionary opportunity in Japan had my name on it.

Reflecting upon my summers as an educator, I rehearsed how I not only earned my Master of Arts degree in English at Bread Loaf School of English, an international and distinguished English language school in Vermont, part of the Middlebury College Language Schools, but also I conducted a Gospel choir while a senior citizen student there. No one could convince me that I did not have everything I needed to be selected for this missionary assignment in Tokyo. I would not need the language to begin my missionary journey there in Japan because I would later learn the language in connection with my English/clergy tasks.

Kathi's enthusiasm matched my excitement. Her cheerful disposition landed both of us laughing at how much we wanted to make this first assignment work for me. She shared that I seemed quite suitably equipped and we forged ahead. I looked forward to becoming the answer to the request at our Church of God academic school in Tokyo.

Though I enjoyed some meaningful ministry tasks at my church and in a few other venues for a while, I felt weary that twelve years had passed and I had yet to experience a vocational career in ministry. I mused--so what if I had matriculated in seminary at the tender age of 50 and graduated at 53 in 2000. So what if I were approaching my 65th birthday in April of 2012. I felt young at heart. As a highly energized, committed, creative, and enthusiastic woman of the gospel, ordained and committed, Tokyo and I should make a strong connection and go forth with English language achievements and anticipated ministry outcomes. With Kathi as my coach, we worked together tirelessly and harmoniously trusting that this assignment offered a nearly perfect end to my 12 year trek for a ministry placement. Without the critical spiritual equipping of sister girls, perhaps I might have abandoned my vision for the mission field. These devout prayer partners: Pauline Vivian Green Staggers, [Vivian] Rev. Gloria N. Adams, Pastor Suzanne Haley, Deacon Barbara Lewis, Sister Connie Phillips and our treasured small group among others served as angels on loan in my life. Their presence, particularly during this time of God's testing my faith, refreshed my journey. Vivian Staggers and I, in 2021, are now nearing thirty years of faithful praying for and with one another for an unending list of prayer needs. Rev. Gloria taught me an approach to the scriptures that quenched my thirst for the practical application of God's word.

As my bible teacher and prayer partner, Gloria established and maintained a small group known as Adam's Portion. Under her tutelage, we experienced exponential growth both as a small group and as individuals. Deacon Barbara [deceased 2020] was my Small Group leader and prayer partner who modeled selflessness and patiently taught me the same. Her deferential treatment of the body of Christ inspired not only her small group, but also her family, neighbors and all who knew and loved her. Deacon Barbara cared for my home in my multiple summer absences and in my academic year in Yap, Micronesia. These women--along with too many others to name--walked with me through all of my missionary journeys over an eight year period. Their leadership example inspired me to overcome adversities during what seemed to have been a 12 year holding pattern. These sisters sacrificed energy and time regularly to hold up my arms along my path. My gratitude to them ends at heaven's gate. Great is their reward from God alone. I remain indebted to them.

Meanwhile, Kathi and I kept tracking our Tokyo details. One day my telephone rang and I heard Kathi's voice and knew immediately that she needed to share disappointing news. Neither she nor I found ourselves prepared for the reason that the Tokyo school did not accept me. In their cultural context, as a 65 year old, I no longer qualified for their program. Though at the time of my application, I was still only 64 years old, turning 65 while in the assignment was unacceptable. Kathi felt that she had taken so much time with me and had inspired me and made such significant arrangements that she apologized profusely for not being made aware of the age issue.

I told her that God would make up to both of us our hopes for my first missionary assignment.

Going Forward

A year later [2013], Kathi called me again and advised me that Yap, Micronesia did not have an age issue. Yap International Christian School needed a clergy/teacher to fulfill a yearlong assignment for the career missionaries that would return to their native Canada to continue friend-raising, which ensures that they will have sufficient funding to sustain their assignment in Yap. Without hesitation, I accepted the assignment believing wholeheartedly that God sent it to me. Kathi committed to train the number of first time missionaries at our headquarters. She shared various texts that I needed to read. She planned a weekly tutorial with me using one of the texts written from a previous missionary's experience in Yap, Micronesia. What a richly rewarding experience.

Alas, I submitted to the grind of re-organizing my life to be away for one year. Little did I appreciate the demands of friend raising. This term refers to the need for missionaries to inspire widespread friendships that resulted in committed financial support for one's missionary assignments. In the instance of a short term assignment, the on-going budget for your current residence must be considered. Ideally, a tenant in your home lessens the related expenses of sustaining your property in your absence. If a tenant does not appear, one must now sustain two lifestyles—one at home and one on the mission field. Our CHOG Global Strategy requires missionaries to raise 100% funding for their missionary budget. This aspect of the preparation seemed quite daunting to me. Nonetheless, in a series of workshops and one-on-one sessions, Kathi Sellers poured into all of us as first assignment missionaries and instructed us on how to master friend-raising.

Furthermore, we needed to study our respective countries and become culturally literate for our good success. Kathi and her husband spent nearly two decades on the mission field in Latin America.

Kathi's infectious enthusiasm stimulated her novice group of commissioned missionaries and instilled confidence in us. After the overwhelming support of my home church, Celebration Church at Columbia, with our then Lead Pastor and First Lady, Robbie and Robin Davis and the entire church family supporting the friend-raising, I gained momentum. Other churches in our Chesapeake, Delaware and Potomac district followed my home church's example lending their financial support needed to get this budget to 100%. A few years earlier, I befriended our Winning Women's Conference speaker, Lady Meredith Sheppard of Destiny Church in California. As a result of our sisterhood and upon her request, her husband, Pastor Paul Sheppard, decided to have Destiny Church match the contribution of Celebration Church at Columbia. My former and second home church, Third Street Church of God under the leadership of Pastor Cheryl J. Sanders offered not only financial support but technological devices that I continue to enjoy today. Personal friends and prayer partners supported my former landlady, Tonya McKinney, who planned a bus trip to New York to raise enough money to strengthen my budget. My heart continued to be deeply touched by the bubbling up of energy by my church families, friends and neighbors who could not believe that I would journey alone so far from home in my senior years to share as a missionary in such an unknown land as Yap, Micronesia.

In the final days before I reached my budget, I felt distressed. My budget was not quite two thirds complete with an August destination date in view. Just a few weeks remained and from my perspective, I exhausted my resources. A lifetime friend, Cheryl Broadway and her mom, Mother Ethel Wooden invited me to join them on a vacation trip to Cape May, New Jersey in July 2013. I love the water and needed this trip. In this way, I threw caution to the wind, left the multiple tasks that remained and joined my friends en route to Cape May. We drove our car onto the ferry--second to cruising, crossing from state to state on the ferry--fascinates me. There we were in Delaware waiting in line, car in tow, safe on the ferry. Quickly, Cheryl and I skipped steps to the upper deck and arrived on the first level to watch the ferry lumber along like weary sea lions as the ferry carried all that weight (some thirty or more cars) and some 60 or 70 passengers across the waters to Cape May. I engaged the captain of the ferry in a discussion about the dynamics of weight in the water and what makes it happen. Such an experience captivated me. He patiently explained the physics and other related issues of how this ferry carried all the cars and humans to their destination. I remain awed by this fun-filled activity that I longed to experience more often.

After a day and a half of fun along the beach in Cape May spotting the dancing dolphins and enjoying the antics of toddlers digging in the sand, I released my tensions regarding my budgetary woes for this first and promising missionary assignment. I surrendered believing that God guides and provides. Why God seemed to be taking such a great while to provide this budget no longer troubled me. I knew that my faith must not only bear up under the pressure, but also increase in depth and breath. I need to trust God for the outcome of this friend-raising. The next day, while her mom napped, Cheryl and I went to the outdoor hot tub to lounge in the heated waters. Upon our return to the room, Cheryl asked me to quiet my spirit and sit with her. She then prayed passionately about my friend-raising woes. We felt the presence and power of God in that room. Cheryl remains an intercessory prayer warrior to this day and I believe in her faith-filled prayer ministry. About two minutes after we prayed, my cell phone rang. On the other end was the bubbling voice of Debbie Taylor, another Global Strategy staff member who encouraged me along with Peggy Beverly and Candace Power as we anticipated that somehow I would soon be budget secured and en route to Yap. Debbie shared with me that Christian Women's Connection under the leadership of their then Director, Dr. Arnetta McNeese Bailey, submitted a check to my required budget. The dollar amount took me over the 100% funding mark. Cheryl, her mom and I could not stop praising God for this miracle. Cheryl is a praise dancer and she danced like David and filled the room with infectious joy. Her mom and I felt the faith-filled jubilation in that hotel suite. We left that suite with the residue of profound joy in my life that day.

In the final hours before my flight to Yap, Micronesia, I sat on the stairs in my townhouse, staring at the carpet that by then had been walked upon by many different feet. At least a dozen friends from the church came and went. Each dear soul offered gracious assistance to get this senior citizen up and away on her solo journey to Yap. I managed to rent my home to a single male tenant. Regrettably, he remained in my home twelve months but only paid the rent for two. That left me in quite a financial dilemma. Nonetheless, because I trusted all of my affairs to my faithful friend, Barbara. I asked her not to quarrel with him for the rent. I cautioned her that her 6'6" son, if he learned of an unpleasant encounter between her and my tenant from whom she sought the rental fee, he, at 6' 6" may feel compelled to introduce himself to the tenant. I did not want the remote possibility of such an encounter. I left the tenant with an organized home hopefully that he enjoyed in spite of his neglect.

Nonetheless, I digress. Back to my weary soul. With the budget settled, the house organized for the tenant, and my documents in order for the journey, I failed to reach my packing goals. From the crown of my head to the soles of my feet, my body now felt just like a washing machine that gave all, then broke down and dismantled right smack in the middle of the most important last cycle of critical wearing apparel. Oh wow, I could hardly lift my arms. I discovered that I put every ounce of energy into everything except packing my bags. Now needing to take at least minimal items, exhaustion nearly paralyzed me. Suddenly I feared the worse. I would not be ready in just a few hours for my transportation to the airport. I considered just walking out the door with my handbag, one change of clothes and my technological devices. I dropped my head into my lap and slapped my hands across the back of my neck. Though I had planned to pack five times earlier, things just kept interfering with that task. Crestfallen and sleep deprived, I sat on my steps at 1:30 am absolutely OUT of energy. I could not lift my arms or legs anymore. I had no bags packed, no rest or sleep for several days, and my wake-up call was fast approaching. I feared oversleeping and throwing my travel arrangements into a chaotic mess. I asked myself, "how did you get into such a predicament?"

Alas, I held my face in my hands, massaged my temples, stretched my upper torso, rocked back and forth on the steps and began to pray. I felt like a discarded dishrag that had washed hundreds of dishes and plopped on the counter, discolored and tattered. All my drained energy draped over my body like the X-ray apron at the dental office. Finally, I asked God to calm my spirit for just 30 minutes, then energize me by the Holy Spirit. I then needed God to carry me up my stairs and miraculously pack--through me--only those things urgently needed in Yap. Once again, God's love manifested in extravagant evidence. I took a 30 minute power nap holding the pegs in the railing of my steps to keep me aware that I was not in bed. Finally, I lifted my left leg and then my right one. I pulled myself up by the guardrail of my stairs. I wiggled and waddled myself up the stairs and lifted a piece of luggage in my packing room. I stilled my body and emotions and I asked God to speak to me. I threw the luggage across the bed, prayed to God again and asked God to guide me to ONLY the essentials for this journey. In a desperate attempt to pack one bag, I vowed that wearing the same two or three ensembles everyday for the entire 10 months no longer occupied my mind. The Holy Spirit directed me to take a shower first to wake up and not collapse on the floor. I then attacked the top ten or fifteen items that I needed in Yap. I experienced a burst of energy after I packed for a few minutes. I looked at my packing list prepared several days earlier and realized that I could pack a few more items as I anticipated attending a variety of events overseas. I packed my three bags--two for checking and one for inside the aircraft. I trusted that I could sustain myself for 10 months with these items.

Unbelievably, I actually bounded down the steps at 5:30 am, one piece of luggage in hand, two others with which my friends would assist me. My friends expressed amazement that I just had two checked bags. I told them that a third checked bag cost $200.00. They laughed and said: "oh that kind of fee will make you travel light." We hopped into the car and headed to Baltimore Washington's Thurgood Marshall International airport. I sang to myself: "What a mighty God we serve." My friends drove quietly taking in the early morning air. We laughed about how life looked at 5:30 in the morning.

We arrived at the International terminal and prepared for the baggage check. One friend went to park in the lot while the other looked for assistance for me. Now in a dazed state of mind, I needed guidance and direction to process my several flights ahead. My energy waned; momentarily, I nearly forgot where I was going. Suddenly an airport staff member approached me. His kind, gentle manner quickened in me the need to share my documents. I explained that my level of exhaustion rendered me nearly motionless. The kind gentleman said to me: "I will take good care of you." I will get a wheelchair for you, check your bags and take you all the way through security to your departing gate. I sighed and thought this angel dropped into the terminal from the heavens above. My friend requested a guest pass to accompany me to the gate. We then made our way through throngs of international late August travelers and arrived at my departing gate. Tearfully, I thanked both my friend and the kind stranger. I shared a gratuity with him and offered a blessing as well. Unbelievably, I got it all done. For this great God is my God forevermore.

I walked curiously through the aircraft to the economy section–gosh someday I hope to travel business class–found my seat, plopped into it and went straight to a sound sleep in just 30 seconds. Even though the tight, uncomfortable economy seats seemed to be the tax that long-legged poor people had to pay, I needed sleep so badly that I simply accepted our frustratingly cramped conditions. At least I had the aisle seat that I requested for my osteo-arthritic right knee. I trusted God to alert me when the jumbo jet landed. From Baltimore's Thurgood Marshall International airport to Honolulu, Hawaii, I tried to keep my neck from feeling the pressure of my bobbing head. This sleep knew no boundaries. All dignity disappeared. I went to dreamland. Kind seatmates nudged me at mealtimes. Immediately after eating, I drifted back into newborn baby sleep. From Honolulu, we flew to Guam. When I finally arrived in Guam, my career missionary colleague, Pastor Gary Bistritan, waited at customs for me. What a wonderful sight to see him and to know that he would assist me with the 10 hour layover before our flight from Guam to Yap. Friends in Guam, who often provided a respite for the Yap night-time flight travelers, once again received Pastor Bistritan and now me. We enjoyed rest time, a scrumptious meal and sightseeing before the midnight flight. I confess–I lifted my hands to the heavens for this 36 hour journey and the safety I experienced all along the way. Are you familiar with Yap, Micronesia in the South Pacific Islands? None of my family and friends knew about Yap. I later learned that, in fact, an adventure seeking nephew of mine actually had visited and done some snorkeling in Yap. That so pleasantly surprised me. I talk about Yap everywhere I go because it is a most exotic and inviting adventure for all.

Both Pastor Gary Bistritan and his wife Gwen are 30 year career missionaries. They founded a lovely school for grades kindergarten to 8th grade--Yap International Christian School [YICS]--and the school, I am advised, has now doubled in size and attendance and is thriving on that 6,000 person island. What a joy to see our two story compound that is set directly across the street on one side from a Mormom Worship Center with a backyard basketball court; and on the other side a Yap elementary public school with beautiful grounds. Every day I kept my eye on that public school wondering if someday our Yap ICS would transfer over to that expanse and meet more of our students' needs. My teaching tasks inspired me to give my all to these beautiful kindergarten children. Our school used the Accelerated Christian Education [ACE] curriculum. I received the training to use this material in Tennessee, one of the headquarters for the ACE curriculum development and teacher training. My other tasks involved serving as the interim principal of our school, teaching music, training a choir, and teaching bible study. Our building supported both our school and church--Yap International Church of God. My days in Yap transformed my life. The splendid opportunity to use more of my skills blessed my life. Though we experienced some turbulence in our approach to educating these precious island students, I met my professional, personal and spiritual goals. Conflict brought compassion on all sides and offered us the privilege of modeling the character of Christ for all of the Yap family.

The Bistritans returned to Yap mid-January 2014. After a wonderfully well planned Christmas program by our staff and parents, I journeyed to Manila, Philippines to meet the Virays. Pastor Eddie and Dr. Fely Viray had a lovely family and they all lived in a compound in an area of Manila thought to be dangerous. I was never permitted to leave the compound without one of my Filipino family members. On the mission field, you become family straightaway. You arrive, meet and greet, share a meal, and throw yourself into the routine offering support and assistance as needed. You are family. It happened in Yap and now in the Philippines as well. In the Philippines I probably learned as much in the two weeks there than I learned in a year elsewhere. The Virays managed a demanding schedule for their Christmas activities. We rose early and began serving the families of God and the community with Christmas joy, programs and presents. I never stopped smiling and absorbing such generosity among the most gracious people. Their love and kindness arrested me. The Virays and my experience in Manila left an indelible impression in my spirit and a giant sized fingerprint on my soul.

Upon my return to Yap, I met the two young adult volunteers that Pastor Gary and Gwen brought with them. These two young people changed the energy of our school. They could do all kinds of things that I once did when my physical body allowed it. I reveled in the energy of their interactions with our students. Gwen and the two young adults and I shared kitchen duties. Gwen cooked scrumptious meals from scratch and surprised us with delectables. We, now as a family, enjoyed cultural excursions around and about Yap as well as Guam. I admired the patience of Job that Gwen exhibited every day of our time together. She wore many hats. After she prepared breakfast in the morning, she taught kindergarten in the afternoon. She supported the administrative tasks of her husband and was the pianist for our music program and church services. This dear sister taught me everything I needed to know about kindness for hers remained unrelenting from the day that we met until the last time that I saw her at a missions conference in Chiang Mai, Thailand in March 2017. Gwen's sisterly devotion like the Virays humbled me. She impressed upon me the deep and abiding need to serve selflessly, patiently and non-judgmentally. What a delightful soul to know and love in the person of Gwen Bistritan.

God's extravagant evidence in my travels to Yap, Guam, Manila, Tokyo and surrounding areas during that academic year raised the bar for my spiritual growth. I struggled to express my gratitude to those who made this journey possible. I grappled with words that might express my gratitude to our Southeast Asia/South Pacific Island missionary supervisors in the persons of Don and Caroline Armstrong. These two career missionaries gave me their undivided attention during my stay in Yap. We worked through sensitive conflicts, communication breakdowns, stress management issues and cultural literacy matters. Their patience with this senior citizen missionary, who wanted to rearrange some things, reinforced in my mind how much God loved me. God's grace and mercy expressed through Don and Caroline Armstrong continued through my missionary assignment in Chiang Mai, Thailand in 2017. Don and Caroline are seasoned missionaries having served in Africa for some sixteen years. In their role as missionary supervisors in Southeast Asia, they oversee the ministries of missionaries and their projects in twenty-two nations.

I embraced a family during that school assignment and in October 2021, the two oldest boys–who were among my students at our School for Success in Chiang Mai–successfully completed their GED requirements and received their certificates. Because the three boys--the youngest one will enter high school next year--and their family was on the United Nations High Commissioner for Refugees [UNHCR] list, I intervened on their behalf. While I could not get the attention of the State department, immigration lawyers in the USA or Vice President Mike Pence, the family realized that I made major efforts to assist them in their resettlement. Remember that I told you in a preceding paragraph how much I try to rearrange things in our world and make them what I believe they ought to be. The UNHCR gently reminded me in writing that the process that I followed would not result in the family being resettled until their number came up and they met the appropriate conditions for resettlement. Well, in October 2021, by a miracle of God--all refugee families do not get resettled in the West--this family safely arrived in Canada after nearly ten years of waiting, holding, petitioning, pleading and making their case. I remain connected to this family and I expect to support all three sons in their pursuit of higher education either in Canada or the USA.

I am a transformed creature after Yap, Thailand, and Hungary where I served the needs of students who wish to study and master the English language. Because I have a theatrical background and classical vocal training, I enjoyed teaching my students music from both the African and African-American traditions. I never imagined that my life would evolve into international missions beginning in Fortaleza, Brazil in 1999 to Torokszentmiklos, Hungary in 2019. I bow in humble submission to our God who allowed me to grow, blossom, and mature in Christian service by taking me across the world and back on many different occasions. Such extravagant evidence of God's love ignites within me an unquenchable fire. Wherever God leads, I must tell my story. Thank you for both reading and sharing this book.

Vermont Vitality–1

Delight thyself also in the Lord: and he shall give thee the
desires of thine heart. Psalm 37:4 —King James Version

In August 1989, I headed for Heathrow airport after a stunningly beautiful summer of study in Oxford, England at the Wycliffe Hall campus. As a DC Public School teacher, eager to advance in my profession, I won a grant from the Morris and Gwendolyn Cafritz Foundation to participate in a noteworthy east coast's summer program at Wycliffe Hall in Oxford. I could have turned backward somersaults in iron chains because this seemed to be such an unbelievable opportunity for this southern country girl from Texas. Quite an unreachable goal for the lassie from San Antonio who still longed for love, romance, marriage and the big family headed by a strong husband surrounded by a doting wife and mother living in a large brick house with a wrap-around porch, an expansive backyard with both vegetable and flower gardens. I anticipated running across the lawn all day everyday with my children who soaked up the love of their parents and siblings as they came of age in San Antonio, Texas. Alas, none of that activity occurred, so education consumed my time. The privilege of studying in Oxford, England quite fascinated my mom. I felt affirmed that maybe my mental acuity warranted this honor. At Wycliffe Hall, I met my colleagues who arrived from different states in the USA and intended to pursue their Master's and doctoral degrees in the field of rhetoric with an emphasis on writing.

Our program stimulated much interest among American teachers.

After a delightful summer filled with frequent excursions to London and the countryside of England, I completed my demanding course work and headed for the airport. Perhaps the greatest thrill of my final days in Oxford was the arrival of my 75 year old mom who longed to visit England and France. She studied literature from both countries and had read volumes of history about both nations. We enjoyed a splendid seven day journey through London, Oxford and then on to Paris and the countryside of France. What a refreshing experience for my mom. She complained of no aches or pains as we walked for many hours each day of our time in both England and France. Mom enjoyed the Bed and Breakfast accommodations and wanted to show our hosts her great pleasure by being their most enjoyable guests. I got so tickled at how she engaged them in pithy conversations about their country. They loved chatting with her. I had hoped that she and I could fly together. Nevertheless, she returned to Texas and I returned to Washington, DC. Both she and I had obligations back in our respective locales.

When I arrived at Heathrow, I met a young woman in the lobby who had completed her summer study at Bread Loaf School of English [BLSE] at their Oxford, England campus. As we discussed our two programs that focused upon the teaching of writing through reading, listening, thinking and speaking tasks, I inquired more extensively about her program at Bread Loaf. She stated emphatically that in her opinion, the BLSE program was superior to what I just experienced through another noteworthy east coast university. She advised me to not only apply to BLSE, but also to earn my Master's degree in English there. I did just that! But, let me tell you about the effect of the state of Vermont on my holistic health.

I began my journey at Bread Loaf after having won a second National Endowment for the Humanities grant to the state of Vermont. The first one was at St. Michael's College in Colchester [the suburbs of Burlington, Vermont.] I sensed something unusual and special about the Green Mountain state of Vermont. I later learned that Vermont never supported slavery and its soil did not know the horrors of that kind of human treatment. This first grant through the National Endowment for the Humanities–with whom I forged a two decade long relationship–winning grant after grant focused our studies upon "Boethius: The Consolation of Philosophy" and

J.B., the play. These texts: "Job, Boethius and J.B." occupied most of the daylight hours for the fifteen teachers/scholars from across the nation. Our living accommodations in the apartments for students at St. Michael's offered us private bedrooms and sufficient kitchen, living room and dining room space. I loved living with my two roommates: one a former Catholic nun, and the other a Philadelphia high school teacher.

In anticipation of an intellectually demanding summer, I chose to drive to Vermont from my home in Washington, DC. In 1987, I used AAA [the American Automobile Association] to prepare a trip ticket for me. I followed the Interstate through upstate New York and finally came to the state of Vermont. I then began to follow the paths of two lane roads sprawling, winding, rounding curves, up and down hills with picturesque landscapes and a panoramic view of the green mountains. What was this I sensed in the atmosphere? Why did I feel so refreshed, so free, so relaxed and so unafraid? Along the Interstate in New York, I sensed a different kind of energy: hustle/bustle lessened greatly by nature's aesthetic, but nonetheless, cars traveling sometimes miles above the speed limit seemingly with urgent deadlines awaiting them at multiple destinations. Not so in this Green Mountain state of Vermont. I found the driving to be calming. I could think as I gazed upon the mountaintops, imagining myself climbing the mountains.

What did I sense here? Suddenly it dawned upon me. Something genuinely different about this air in Vermont. The countryside scenery punctuated what awakened my five senses. I felt personally, socially and emotionally FREE. I felt relaxed. I sensed that I did not have to FIGHT against being invisible. For the first time in all of my travel experiences across the USA: midwest, southeast, northeast, northwest, west coast, and southernmost regions of the country, though joyful, sometimes pleasant, sometimes intense, sometimes unsettling, sometimes refreshing but NEVER freeing–here in Vermont, I felt free. I remember going to sleep at night in hotel/motel rooms, my own homes, homes of others and saying to myself: relax, breathe deeply, tension is mounting in your body. In Vermont, I relaxed in my accommodations for graduate students at each facility during my five summers there. Each summer of my studies, I traveled alone across Vermont's awe inspiring landscape. I remember how often I breathed deeply and rested well in motels as I criss-crossed the land of Green Mountains. Why was Vermont different? I learned that Vermont did not have slaves and supported the underground railroad. I visited one of the most often used underground railroad sites. From my perspective, I wondered how did Vermont become identified as such a wholesome place for the quality of human life?

I spent some five years going and coming to Vermont in the summertime. I considered relocating to Vermont to teach in either middle or high school. A colleague sat me down and talked with me about the weather in Vermont. He explained that most likely the winters would last from late October to early April or thereabout. This weather report became a deal breaker for me. This southern belle needed much more warm air than Vermont provided during their early winter and late spring season.

Thus, my trade off was the five summers that I spent there. My memories of Vermont remind me of what possibilities exist in the human family and in the USA. We, humans, can behave in a civil manner with one another all day, everyday. In fact, we, humans, can treat each other with respect and dignity. I experienced it in Vermont. That means that it can happen. It can be done. We can sustain healthy attitudes toward another dear soul. I believe that by an act of our will, we can embrace our fellow humans with a strong sense of let's do life together in our jobs, in our communities, in the marketplace, and in our recreational spaces. Sometimes I observe the most stunningly beautiful behavior by my fellow humans. On other hand, when we behave in a grotesquely inhumane way, it speaks volumes to all of us. Quick question—why do our pets love us unconditionally? What can we learn from them? Can we work intentionally to behave better toward one together? Yes we can. If it is happening in Vermont, it means that it can happen everywhere. I believe that It is an act of the human will. Far too simplistic an offering, I know.

Far too simplistic. I am gullible, I am told. I look at life through rose-colored glasses, I am told. I am an idealist, I am told. I am such a melancholy, emotionally charged person, I am told. I constantly speak in hyperbole, I am told. I will take all of those characterizations…those words that used to cause me to feel marginalized, weird, subnormal, childish, foolish, and even frightened that I would never become a person who offers enough to the world to be noticed in an authentic way. I need to become more realistic, more accepting of the world as it is–I am told–I need to accept life's reality. Vermont taught me to resist accepting things as they are and to work for change. I began this journey in 1987 and I continue it today. Change is beautiful!

This is the issue: Civility says that one cannot be quiet… without recognizing the dignity and worth of fellow humans. Such dignity and worth acknowledged through neighborly behavior and community bonding surely improves the quality of our daily coming and going in our world. I, however, recognize the limits of civility. We humans have multiple personal and emotional issues compounded by how we were shaped culturally, politically, spiritually and emotionally. In this way, God showed me unconditional LOVE and demonstrated through outrageous evidence how this kind of LOVE brought me internal peace, exceeding joy, bragging rights [no boast except in Christ] and wholesome relationships with members of the human family.

Vermont took me to an all time high as I enjoyed the pastoral scenes of the countryside in all of New England. I respected my colleagues. I mastered the coursework. I enjoyed making new friends. I grabbed the opportunity, when asked, to form a gospel choir at Bread Loaf School of English. We soared in the two concerts that we presented. What a loving experience–gospel music at Bread Loaf in the mountains. Wow! I completed my Master's degree in English and I drove down the mountains feeling a burst of humanity that sustained me throughout my entire teaching career in the years ahead. Once again, this experience demonstrated extravagant evidence of God's perfect love for me. Planning to explore the New England countryside alone as well as earning a degree in Vermont never entered my mind while tackling teaching tasks in DC Public Schools. The entire experience tickled my insides and caused me to blush as I gazed upon the heavens. I love Vermont. I am not disillusioned there. No, not at all.

Hungary Heals

*"Humble yourselves therefore under the mighty hand
of God, that he may exalt you in due time."*
I Peter 5:6—King James Version

When did you last visit Yap, Micronesia? What about Torokszentmiklos, Hungary? You've never heard of these places! Oh no. Well, let me take you to my most recent experience with what may be unfamiliar places to my readers. In my essay titled Missionary Miracles, I share my experiences in Yap, Micronesia. In this essay, I want you to know all about my life-extending experiences in Hungary—from my arrival to my departure—my everyday experiences in Hungary satisfied a deep longing in my soul for quiet rest, recovery, and resolve. I knew that God arranged both Hungary and specifically Torokszentmiklos, a village in the countryside of Hungary, for a much needed time of refreshing for me. I confess that at the end of the summer of 2019, I found myself to be a weary soldier in the army of the Lord. I needed respite, revival, and rest.

I arrived in Budapest, Hungary after I received a sudden and unexpected English teaching opportunity offered to me on Friday, July 19, 2019. A rushed interview with guest educators from Budapest, Hungary on that early Saturday morning, July 20th; followed by a fast moving contract agreement and photo opp on Monday, July 22nd, thereby interrupting all my plans to relocate to San Antonio, Texas stopped me in my tracks. My question to God remained—God are you in this entire situation? I desperately desire to avoid another misstep. All of this sudden activity and these radical changes in my plans followed the cold and dreary experience of losing my home in Columbia, Maryland. How could my missteps result in such a great loss. At one point, I worked four different jobs to afford the original mortgage on my home. I loved that townhouse on a semi-circle inner court off the major street that afforded me assigned front door parking. My home provided solace and many times of refreshing for me, my visiting family and friends. This God-given home allowed me to share space with my sister girls in our small group commitment. My cousin, Yvonne, thought that my living room looked like a jungle. She's so funny. She felt overwhelmed by the sprawling and thriving house plants that punctuated my intimate and simple living room environment. I loved these healthy, crawling Ivy Golden Pothos plants. They were my children speaking life to me from every horizontal space in my living room. Nonetheless, that awful summer, much to my chagrin, my home ownership landed me in the "Short Sale" process. Then, suddenly, an unexpected opportunity arrives in Eastern Europe. Only God knew the quality of healing that the nation of Hungary would bring into my life. More of God's extravagant evidence of such pure and perfect love for this love-thirsty dear soul.

What happened suddenly now took "suddenly" to another level. Unbelievably, a month after the whirlwind activities in July, along with all of my abrupt and disruptive change of plans, I received an unsettling email regarding my trip. On August 19, 2019, a few days before my departure date, I received an email from my fellow Hungarian educators that advised me to postpone my arrival date to Budapest, Hungary until August 2020. Since my plans to teach school in Hungary came suddenly and unexpectedly as detailed above, I had already detoured on the road to Texas. I thought that I could teach in Hungary for a few years. I shared my new opportunity with my siblings, my church family, and my friends far and near. Too, I disbursed my earthly possessions to multiple charities, neighbors and beloved friends who would appreciate them. Before this email, I reflected upon becoming conversational in the Hungarian language. I pondered the many steps needed to improve my teaching skills to non-native English speakers. I contemplated how much I could enjoy not only Eastern Europe's rich history and culture, but also how I could travel around and about a few other European nations. Having met my lovely Hungarian educators in the conference room of the Veritas Collegiate Academy in Fairfax, Virginia with the Elguts, both I and Maria Elgut considered me to be an answer to prayer. Maria Elgut, Superintendent of Grammar Schools at Veritas contacted me through a Zip Recruiter resume. She spoke so rapidly during our initial conversation on that God-given Friday in July that I believed she must have heard from God. From my perspective, everything was settled and I made all of the adjustments. My confidence in God's plan fueled my curiosity. A year's delay could not be the will of God. A year's delay would create more chaos for me. A year's delay saddened me deeply. In retrospect, a year's delay probably would never happen for me considering the world pandemic and my sibling's earnest request that I remain stateside for a few years until the pandemic seemed much less treacherous—especially for senior citizens.

This email requesting a hold on our commitment needed my immediate attention. At the risk of behaving like an "ugly American," I tried to gently persuade my Hungarian colleagues not to change the plans for my arrival in Hungary. I communicated to them how much faith I had in God to turn this situation into a blessing for some students there in Hungary. I did not want to alienate myself with them. I spoke to Maria Elgut and perhaps she spoke with them to seek a better alternative than a year's postponement. For a moment I feared that the Hungarian colleagues would just move on from my issues and go forward with their request. Afterall, what could I do if they simply could not honor my request? In an act of compassion, I believe, not only did they keep the reservation in place, but also because of a medical emergency with my health, I requested respectfully that they even change my departure date to 48 hours later than the original date. Little do they know, even now, that they have made a lifetime friend in me. As my life unfolds, I will not forget their many acts of kindness toward me. They honored all of my requests. This story continues.

An Apology for Wholesome International Relations

I explained to my Hungarian colleagues the reality of my situation. I shared with them how my church and three of the women's bible studies to which I belonged had celebrated my new adventure and had generously given support monies to encourage me on this journey. Turning back jarred my central nervous system. Suddenly this change sounded like the bongs and vibrations of timpani drums pounding throughout my head. No turning back could possibly occur. In my perception, trying to explain an "oops" moment to supporters of missionaries only creates a breach. No explanations seem safe when people accept your presentation for missionary support. In this way, I knew I must go to Hungary. Most of my earthly possessions now had new homes. I wanted to give myself away in complete service to the children in Hungary. I needed to become completely unencumbered by my middle class lifestyle. So much pressure seemed to bear down on my already stressed shoulders. I wanted to apologize to my Hungarian colleagues for not being more patient with their needs and focusing entirely on my need. I wanted our international relations to be healthy. I needed my Hungarian colleagues to think of me with a smile and not with eyes rolling up in the top of their head. I apologized a few times over. They accepted my apology.

Finally, on that Saturday evening in August 2019, after many personal and business details were left in the hands of my faithful sister girls, I threw the last bags for my journey in my niece's overcrowded compact car. Now, my niece, and I rumbled along the dimly lit heavily traveled Beltway on Interstate 495 in northern Virginia sensing an awakening due to a sudden turn of events for both of our lives. My niece and I spent such fulfilling quality time together traveling around and about the DMV, [District of Columbia, Maryland and Virginia suburbs] that I bowed my head in sadness at the possibility of missing her greatly. We laughed and entertained the idea of her going away with me. For a moment, that idea nearly took on a life of its own for she, too, stated that she did not know what she would do with my being so far away from home. Before the drive to Dulles ended that evening, she and I reflected upon how intensely busy the group of us were in the final hours of packing, shipping, organizing, arranging, the remaining items in my house. It felt scary as the hour approached to travel to the airport considering the many details that still demanded attention. Alas, I knew that my friends felt committed to assist my niece and one another in caring for the business at hand soon after I boarded the aircraft to Europe. Somehow the final hour with my niece felt surreal. The incident-free drive to the airport represented the longest road traveled from my former home to a new day dawning in a foreign land—the unknown, the unexpected, the language barriers, the new friends, the culture, the tasks before me all seemed to loom large like the highest mountains around the world. A couple of "what if" questions tried to steal my joy.

In retrospect, my heart pounded as I realized how much that I jammed into the thirty days preceding this missionary/teaching assignment—details, details, details—endless details just kept coming at me each new day. Alas, both in my home and one that jumbo jet, I quieted my weary soul looking to the joy of more extravagant evidence of God's perfect love with my life in Hungary. I felt a little alone for a few moments as I sped across the skies in that fully occupied jumbo jet. I looked around for someone with whom I could share a smile. The flight attendant became my new best friend. I drifted into a much needed nap and steadied myself for the ten hour flight to Turkey. I held confidently to my faith that God's perfect love would heal my sadness from the loss of my home and refresh my spirit among a group of people whom I would come to love dearly.

One amusing note—I sure do resent the fleshy squeeze in the ever too tightly, frustratingly uncomfortable "poor folks" compartment—also known as the economy class—of the international flights. Gosh it feels like you get punished for being poor when you take those international flights and we are elbow to elbow for ten or more hours. I am thankful to God that I love people. God, helped me to overcome my resentment when I looked at the legroom of the business class seats. I could not even view the luxury of the first class seats. Oh well, I thought, thank God for safe travels. I rode twice in my life in the first class section of a domestic flight in the USA. Maybe one day I will enjoy a first class international flight. I will then try to share it with someone else who would love such a treat. How annoying to accept that money always makes such a difference in everything—traveling, eating, visiting, working, living... It comforts me to know that it does NOT make the difference in love. God's perfect love freely flows and then we can freely love others with all that God pours into us. That sure makes life worth living. Yes! Money can't buy or sell God's perfect love. Amen.

After breathing deeply and smiling warmly at every dear soul departing the jetcraft, finally, there I stood in the airport baggage claim area in Budapest, Hungary. Nonetheless, I arrived safely and felt delighted when I looked up to see my fellow Hungarian educator waiting for me. She is quite a striking young woman with such a pretty face. She scooped me up at the airport there in Budapest, snatched my three bags, closed the passenger door, drove onto the freeway, pointed out historical places along the stunningly beautiful waterfront with the imposing structures along the drive through Budapest and she soon plopped me into a comfortable and strategically located apartment that offered a scenic view of the Danube River. Whew! She seemed satisfied that both she and I would land a spot for me to earn my keep in Hungary. I meandered about the neighborhood of my apartment complex captivated by the multiple means of transportation available to me: trains, trams, busses, Uber and bicycling on the riverwalk. Though I remained grateful for my arrival in Budapest, I felt anxious about all the details that I left to my niece and friends in my exit from Columbia, Maryland. My sister friends were now empowered to close my house and complete the distribution of my earthly goods. How could I ever get on the other side of this experience, I wondered. I knew that my friends would take good care of everything. They did!

The Back Story—I

I lived in my home in Columbia for fourteen years and had dragged to this lovely townhouse twenty-five years of possessions from my DC, and Cheverly, Maryland homes and my short stay in Laurel, Maryland. I enjoyed my modest townhouse, my attentive neighbors, my walk-friendly community, and my ten years of daily and long term substitute teaching assignments in the Howard County Public School System in Howard County, Maryland. I regretted the Short Sale of my home. I appreciated the joy of dispersing some 98% of my earthly goods to charitable organizations. Sharing momentous gifts and useful home goods with friends, added a greater sense of purpose to my losses. Despair tried to creep upon me for a moment as I accepted the "loss" of thousands of books from my personal library. I won grants for many summers to study both internationally and in the country. I bought books all along the way. I read too little of all of them. Longing to keep some cherished one-of-a-kind gift items soon gave way to the practical aspects of shipping such pieces to San Antonio. In this way, better judgment prevailed. I thanked God that some months earlier than the summer of 2019, I had gifted my former church—Third Street Church of God—with my Boston console piano. I loved it so. It was a beautiful instrument with a grand sound. How I longed to improve my piano skills. Nonetheless, how comforting to know that I would not need the piano or even most of these things in my new home in Hungary. I now embraced the joy of the minimalist lifestyle.

I contemplated my future as I reviewed the five Master's degree programs in which I had matriculated. Three of the five degrees were conferred. The one Master's degree hanging forever in the balance so disturbed my dear Mother that she slumped into absolute disappointment, believing she had given birth to a "quitter." Sigh. I no longer appreciated that I unceremoniously abandoned the first two Master's programs. My array of excuses caused my Mom such distress that I began to understand her profound disappointment in the unfinished degree programs. I made it up to her. Again, it all became more extravagant evidence of God's perfect love in my life. Over a period of fifteen years, I completed not one, nor two, but three Master's degrees; and, my Mom attended all of the graduations with a sense of awe. She seemed particularly overjoyed to attend the graduation from the three year program where I earned the Master of Divinity degree from Princeton Theological Seminary. In the class of the year 2000, with some one hundred students, I was among the only six students in their fifties who graduated. To my astonishing joy, I had been chosen to represent the spirit of the class of 2000 and I won two awards: the Friar's Award [for contributions to the seminary community] and a musical award [for having sung for every aspect of the seminary's life]. Thank God my mom lived to see these graduations. I sang in the choir at the graduation ceremony both at Princeton and in the chamber ensemble at our graduation ceremony at Bread Loaf School of English—Middlebury College, Vermont. As a late bloomer, I thought that I should do everything far above average and beyond reasonable expectations. My mom found great joy in realizing that she did not give birth to a "quitter!" We laughed about that for some time.

After the Princeton celebration, I found myself at 53 years of age, with three Master's degrees and no money, no employment offer that synced with the degrees and no real sense of what in the world should I do next. I probably did not trust God enough because I hurriedly returned to the public school system believing that God may not come through in time for my next budgetary obligation. That misstep cost me hundreds of hours of peace. I got ahead of God. I did not exercise my faith. How could I now believe that God would not come through with a position in vocational ministry? I feared that my age hindered me. I feared that my single status hindered me. I feared that my gender hindered me. I surely became bound by fear. Obviously I feared these issues and more because I did not wait for God to move. I just rushed along and snatched yet another public school teaching position—it was a disaster. Now, I will never know what God had in store for me. That misstep resulted in many hours of agony. Faith requires patience. Patience is short-lived in the life of this Christian woman. Patience is actually short lived in the lives of many other dear souls that I know. My lived experience with my fellow Americans revealed that we will NOT win many or maybe any awards for being a patient people. We live such luxurious lives and patience is not our flavor.

My most painful story about patience takes me to the incident with my tenants in my home in the District of Columbia. While I shared above that I snatched a public school teaching assignment in September 2000, the real truth of the matter is that my impatient tenants drove me to a crazy and quick decision. Following graduation, I actually had a teaching contract in an Episcopal school in Newark, New Jersey. I could not contain my excitement about this contract. I had already identified a pastor and church in Newark, New Jersey as well as living accommodations that suited me just fine. I graduated from seminary now and teaching in this Episcopal school, I thought, would be my first step toward vocational ministry. Then the absolute disgusting impatience of my Catholic University undergraduate student tenants who had demanded a lease from me that suited their terms went unfulfilled. Because of an incident with a gunshot victim that fell dead some 30 feet from my door, my tenants abandoned my home, broke the lease and destroyed some of my furniture. I kept asking, "God, where were you?" I just graduated from seminary and I had such a natural high. I stood on the mountaintop shouting victory in Jesus with my seminary degree, my contract for teaching in a Christian setting, my new church ahead of me and my new life to begin. Alas, the valley was my destiny. That mountaintop experience lasted three short years. The valley of the shadow of death seemed to await me for too long a period to discuss here. Where was my misstep this time?

Here I was with multiple student loans, an empty house for which I now must continue to pay the mortgage, no tenants, a contract that I had to break, the aftermath of a gunshot victim some 30 feet from my door and multiple decisions to make. Why should I be sharing these back stories with my readers? I share them freely because someone needs to know that God's perfect love will put you on the other side of many different valleys of the shadow of death experiences. My story may seem all too simple to some readers who have experienced far more egregious acts in their lives. We humans must appreciate that all pain has its purpose in our lives. My pain wreaked havoc in my life no less than any other nightmare and horror story that I have ever read. I feel nothing but compassion for all of us who have had to endure hardship of any kind. I just know that my pain slowed me to a screeching halt. I felt so exasperated by having to return to DC after my Princeton experience. From my perspective, I needed a fresh start in a different setting. If you have not already read my DC Public School System experience, do read it. You will understand why I wanted to keep it moving after I had been overwhelmingly rejected by the Ward 3 parents of my students in my Advanced Placement classes. I shall nor reiterate the details here. Nonetheless, I thought that God opened the door to the new opportunities in Newark. The return to my emptied home dictated that I now either settle for DC or sweat out trying to begin a new teaching assignment while trying to rent my home, satisfy a new set of tenants and work through those details in my first month of employment in my new school. I did not see this going well for me.

One more reason that I am sharing these two back story episodes with you brings me to this thought: when you travel abroad—perhaps more particularly as a solo traveler—you have precious opportunities to think more clearly. That certainly happened for me every time I traveled abroad to stay for any length of time. Except for England and the South Pacific Islands, I did not have fluency in the languages of my other nations. I laughingly thought of myself as language locked. This allowed me marvelous times for sitting and thinking. What I cherished most in international living was the time that I had to think through my journey. Abroad, I reflected more clearly upon my decision making processes. I studied my scriptures more earnestly. I prayed more diligently. I looked, learned, listened and loved more deeply as I encountered these different cultures and my responses to the people in these countries. I enjoyed rehearsing some of the paths that I followed. I reminisced about the paths that I might have followed. I, soon, concluded that Hungary may never have come to me if I had landed a teaching contract in August 2009 in yet another Christian school after some 25 of us were released in June 2009 from our contracts at Montrose Christian School in Rockville, Maryland. That first week in Budapest allowed for moments of critical reflection upon my spiritual journey, my educational pursuits, my teaching career, my single lifestyle, my ministry opportunities of which I took full advantage in my places of residence in DC and Maryland. Getting away, reviewing my life's journey, and loving my singleness compelled me to ask God to grant wisdom that exceeded zeal. Zeal remained a tour de force with me, but it must now bow to WISDOM and God's wisdom for certain. Missteps should not become a norm, a way of life. Life is far more productive if we can learn to minimize those missteps. I have found it so.

In this way, I anticipated what could happen in Budapest, when to my initial shock, I received a teaching assignment in the countryside of Hungary. My host teacher once again arrived at my Budapest apartment that I very much enjoyed my first week there. She schlepped my luggage and assorted stuff in her economy car, described my school and location, drove me to a drop off point to ride with another colleague, bid me adieu and off I went with a male Hungarian educator whom I just met that morning. It was 5:30am and this colleague who drove me was not in a talking mood. Our two hour trip in silence rather annoyed me. I needed many questions answered. I seemed a bit disoriented for a moment. My colleague drove to the entrance of my new school in the countryside of Hungary in a lovely village named Torokszentmiklos. He then assisted with the emptying of my things from his vehicle, threw his hand of farewell to me; and, I never saw or heard from him again. I wondered why? Could it have been something that I said?

Kolcsey Ferenc Primary School scheduled their school opening ceremony for 8:00 am on Monday, September 2, 2019. I arrived at 7:30 am. I participated with embarrassing yawns because I had been up and about since 4:00 that morning. Soon after my introduction, I trotted off with my new acquaintances to my accommodations, a Bed and Breakfast aka Panzio. Oh no, I had to scale a winding staircase to the 3rd floor. My luggage entered a lift and arrived soon after I dragged my travel weary body to my room. My colleagues trampled all of my earthly goods and neatly arranged them in my new temporary home. The warm, welcoming and most accommodating attitude of our school's Headmaster, Zoli, the dignified faculty, the warm staff and the B&B loving hosts in all of their gracious behavior arrested me. Their kindness endeared me to them immediately. Here I go again,

I thought, experiencing the extravagant evidence of God's perfect love for this struggling 72 year old teacher/missionary. I sometimes wondered if my circuitous route and my multiple missteps to the mission field landed me in such a stunningly beautiful "final" missionary assignment. All of my opportunities as a Special Assignment Missionary [SAM] were solo. I often wondered how things might have unfolded if I had been a part of a team. Nonetheless, each new experience brought exceptional joy and fulfillment to my life.

Before I left Budapest, I reconnected with a cherished colleague in the person of Missionary Carmella Jones, who committed to a five-year assignment in Budapest. I had known her from years past at my Washington, DC church. In Budapest, she and I connected well together—discussing the joys of missionary life in a foreign land with language challenges. Considering our unique status, single, solo African-American female missionaries in Hungary, we began to communicate and live out our compelling journey. Carmella made my life in Hungary sweet, easy, and rewarding. She provided an orientation to my village as only another black woman could do. During a fall break in our school schedule, she and I journeyed to Prague on an overnight train and thoroughly enjoyed touring both Prague and Vienna, Austria. What a glorious teacher's cultural excursion.

We connected with two of Carmella's missionary friends in Prague and attended a church that had the most beautiful oversea, rich velvety red pew cushions that I had ever seen before. The lush cushions and the powerful scarlet color across the expanse of the sanctuary almost distracted me from focusing upon the worship experience. After the service, I remember meeting a lovely South African woman—an Africaner. Perhaps I made a poor judgment call, because I began to discuss the anti-apartheid work with human rights groups that I had done in the USA. She teared up and then began to cry. I suddenly wished that I had exercised more discretion. I could see the pain in her eyes. I quickly changed the subject and offered apologies for that trigger. She explained that it was something that she continued to manage every day of her life. Sigh.

Just a few weeks after our Prague and Austria trips, Carmella invited me to accompany her to Rome, Italy as a special guest to her

American Baptist Missionaries regional conference. I felt incredibly blessed and that invitation once again added to my growing list—another instance of God's extravagant evidence of perfect love for me. The minimal costs of this journey to Rome, my siblings consent to sponsor this missionary conference, the warm welcome by fellow missionaries from a different agency, the great touring adventures around and about Rome rather overwhelmed me. What an unexpected gift from God. Just think, Carmella and I made those several trips in the fall of 2019, just before a world pandemic in March 2020. I still cannot wrap my mind around such extravagant evidence of God's perfect love for an incurable romanticist such as I.

In my final notes about Hungary's sweet fragrance in my life, allow me to share the concluding days in the Panzio and the transition to my final accommodations. My joyful experience with Monica and her hubby found me laughing about extending my stay throughout the school year in their facility just to get those yummy breakfasts every morning. Nonetheless, my flat, a five minute walk from the international train station, was prepared for occupancy. My colleagues scooped up my bags at the Panzio, plopped me into the van with the bags, drove me to the new accommodations—my flat and I sensed the joy of stretching out with my own apartment. When I arrived at my flat, I remember this—from the opening of the front door to the crossing of the threshold, I entered my flat on the "main drag" Almasy Street there in Torokszentmiklos. I loved my flat with the natural sunlight in all four rooms—living room, dining room, kitchen and bedroom. Over the course of my stay, I cherished my view of the nearby homes and the gorgeous sunsets that I witnessed many evenings. The keyed gate to the stairs and the two flights up to this furnished, four room flat satisfied my soul. Imagine just a five minute walk to the train station to travel around and about the region. Nobody but God did this for me. I just wanted to turn backwards somersaults in grand, shiny, bright colored balloons and bubbles of joy. I felt so grateful for this tremendous convenience. I walked throughout the flat every day that I lived there from September 23, 2019 to June 15, 2020 owning its simple beauty and reveling in its charm. Outside each window nature fascinated me with icicles on the trees in the winter and in the spring—abundantly beautiful flower gardens and flowering trees—that lined the boulevard in the springtime. Without any exaggerations, the Europeans grow, arrange and display flowers worthy of significant recognition. I remained wowed by the beauty of their gardens.

The Back Story—II

Negotiating my non-English speaking pastoral, sweet and simple village of 20,000 residents in the countryside—Torokszentmiklos—calmed my soul. I could walk through the neighborhoods and not feel intimidated by the possibility of gun violence. Gun violence in America resulted in my flight from the inner city schools and communities that I deeply cherished in Washington, DC. I never wanted to live outside Washington, DC, but I could no longer manage the gun violence and resulting deaths—once a dear soul fell dead from a gunshot wound some 30 feet from my door. Some weeks later, I saw three different bullet holes in the frame of my front porch window and on my bannister around the porch. In the headlines of the newspapers, as I read the account of the drive by gunshot victims, I felt utterly dismayed. I bowed my head in a sense of frustrating helplessness to prevent this senseless violence my students and I faced in our Washington, DC neighborhoods. Nonetheless, I never ceased to pray. In those early years in Washington, DC, I embraced the beauty of the nation's capital with its historical significance across the earth. I soon became disillusioned with Washington, DC as I learned of one student after another who succumbed to gunshot deaths. Such heartache finally weighed so heavily upon me that I took flight from Washington, DC. I, sometimes, felt guilty. I settled in Columbia, Maryland, a Rouse designed ideal place for families. Though I remained single during my stay there, I found the entire time in Columbia refreshingly enjoyable. Torokszentmiklos, reminiscent of some 99,615 residents of Columbia, allowed me to explore in confidence, walk in safety, and shop in peace. In some ways, Torokszentmiklos, Hungary reminded me of Columbia,

Maryland. Of all the villages in Hungary, only God would send me to Torokszentmiklos. Though my daily and long term substitute teaching experiences in the Howard County Public Schools fulfilled my teaching desire, the insufficient salary resulted in financial distress and the inability to sustain my townhouse in Columbia. In this way, the loss of my home felt like yet another misstep. Good grief! I quarreled with God—how long Lord? Then I remembered Psalm 13 and I silenced my questions and pressed onward!

There in Hungary, I faced a measure of insufficient salary, but I managed to enjoy every aspect of life in Europe. My committed siblings closed the financial gap to ensure that my experiences were free of budgetary limitations. Not only did their financial gifts support my budget, but also I ventured to Vienna, Austria, Prague, Czech Republic, Rome, Italy and Lake Balaton in Hungary. Too, because I find such joy in reflecting upon my experiences in Hungary, I created all kinds of stimulating instructional activities for my primary English language learners. Having taught in high school and middle school for nearly two decades, combined with my primary substitute teaching for a decade in both the USA and internationally, I thought about the challenges of planning lessons for non-native English speakers in the primary grades. At Kolcsey Ferenc, I struggled for a time before I found my sweet spot and a good rhythm as I taught and co-taught in the early childhood and primary classrooms.

Several members of the English staff received their assignments to assist and support me during my tenure at Kolcsey Ferenc. I love their two-syllable names: Kati, my lead teacher, Nati, my walking partner, Brigi, Timi, Judit [Jr.], and Judit [Sr.], such delightful, patient and kind colleagues. We all had the In my teaching tasks at our school, my English teaching colleagues assisted me at every turn. Once Judit Jr. brought me an incredibly delicious fish sandwich—the fish had been caught by her husband. On other occasions I enjoyed fish soup from her husband's fishing trips. Memories of the scrumptious and generous meals prepared by both Judit Sr. and Judit Jr. still bring smiles to my face. Kati graciously prepared for me to eat meals at a wonderful restaurant near my Panzio. Kati treated me to the meals for several weeks. I felt overwhelmingly welcomed and cared for by my Hungarian family. I think of them as family. On the delightful occasion, I recall how our friend Bonnie invited Darby and me to her English speech recital in her home. What a joy to hear the students master the English language. Then there came the celebration and after party of the recital. unending laughter at the after party of that affair. Few words can be shared about the Energy Agi and her son Beni put into making my days in Hungary memorable. Among our thrilling times together, we shared the Chocolate festival, worship service and walks through the village. Agi's husband returned from Germany just in time to ensure that we could ride through the countryside to the Chocolate festival. I stood amazed at the delectables all with a chocolate base.

Nati and her friend, Richard, escorted me to the historic Eger and the day we spent there allowed me to take great photos, purchase lovely souvenirs and experience European pizza at an upstairs cafe. We visited more fun spots along the way. Captivated by the surroundings and the rich history, I tried to take in as much as possible. I have a photo of myself inside one of the cathedrals. That experience sobered me. I always cherish visiting the places of worship. I sense the many prayers that were shared in that solemn space. I became better acquainted with Hungarian culture through this visit to Eger and by spending time with Nati and Richard. The day's adventure warmed my heart. Hungary felt more and more like a little bit of paradise for me after having had such a traumatic farewell in Columbia, Maryland. I chose to give some 98% of my earthly possessions to charitable organizations and friends. I wish I could say that humanitarianism dictated that I do this. I confess that such a gesture occurred because of extenuating circumstances in my life. This outing with Nati and Richard helped me to release so much of the disappointment that I masked during my final days in Columbia. The day's outing reminded me of God's perfect love for me and more extravagant evidence of such perfect love in this stunningly beautiful land so far away from my most immediate experiences that felt like such a miserable misstep in my life. Eger, a historical journey into Hungary's evolution, satisfied my hunger to learn more about Eastern Europe, its people and culture.

I enjoyed the planned meals that my colleagues provided. In the homes of Judit C. and Judit K., I absorbed all of the love, the tasty meals, and the joy of fellowship with them and their family members. I felt honored to be invited into their homes. As a bonus, I enjoyed a recital of spoken English works in the home of Buni. My dear colleague, Darby Runkle, and I journeyed to Szolnok often to enjoy the company of other American teachers in Hungary. Several of them mastered the Hungarian language, married, purchased homes and began families there in Hungary. Wow, I felt inspired. I forged the most delightful friendship with Sue Polgar and our two buddies Ezster and Ilona there in Hungary. We enjoyed many times of food, fun and fellowship with one another. I must someday return to Torokszentmiklos to share again with these lovely bonus sisters in my life. I continue to share on Facebook with Sue, her husband and family. Once again, I am honored to know such lovely human beings in this world. Only God would generously add such love to my life.

Though the school lunch did not work so well for me, I loved to sit in the dining room with the children for a little while. Whenever possible, the lunch staff saved extra beets for me, chicken legs and potatoes. They brought tears to my eyes with their kind gestures to insure that I had something that I could eat every day. The children and I would smile with one another. Unbelievably after months of being in the dining room with them, many of the children behaved as if they were seeing me for the first time. Captivated by their smiles and their pure love, I returned such smiles and felt like my youth was renewed through these experiences. No tonics, no capsules, no treatments of any kind could ever produce in my soul what the love and smiles of these Hungarian children produced. They tenderly reached out to me every day without fail. What an incredibly heart warming embrace. How I wish I could have bottled their love and in liquid form drank of it in the days upon my return to the USA.

After COVID-19 calmed down some, my colleague, Darby, and I spent hours walking and talking all over our village. We did these daily walks for several weeks. Interestingly enough, neither one of us chose to leave Hungary in March after the nation closed down. I told Headmaster Zoli and Lead Teacher Kati that if the world would end now, I would go down with my Hungarian family. They seemed quite surprised that I did not want to rush home. I did not want to leave Torokszentmiklos suddenly. I needed to linger there for a while. I kept experiencing the healing balm that soothed my soul. Toward the end of our stay in Hungary, Darby rented a car, how brave of her, and we ventured to the countryside. My fascination with Hungary reached new heights. Darby and I shared an inter-generational, interracial relationship exploring tough conversations from different perspectives on issues brewing in the USA. We also often swapped stories about our students and school experiences. I bragged so much about my students, colleagues and parents that I probably bored Darby. She patiently listened to the intricate details of my stories and smiled graciously. My love affair with Hungary, its people and my school rather intrigued Darby. I told her that my age probably factored prominently into the extent of my experiences. I mellowed with the years and found myself a more agreeable soul. Regrettably, I noticed some residue of crotchety behavior trying to cling to me. I fought it with a vengeance. Desperate to display God's love, I nearly lost myself in a measure of unattainable perfection. On occasion when I behaved poorly, I apologized profusely. Gosh I wish that I did not struggle with temper trials.

My students did not notice anything about me that they did not like. They kept me dancing on the clouds. Though shyness gripped them in mysterious ways from my perspective, they responded ener-getically to my antics. My colleagues concluded that as their guest, they endured the unorthodox behavior evidenced in the corridors and large meeting rooms. Eager to follow the protocol, my students and I exercised some restraint during our encounters in both the dining room and corridors. Alas, we embraced our emotions, throw-ing kisses and grabbing hugs as we passed one another. I offered apologies to my colleagues that were rewarded with complete accep-tance. My students and I tried to follow the protocol for appropriate school wide behavior but we failed, because hugs and kisses graced the floors, dining room, assemblies, entrances and exits. I loved those children with a wild, uninhibited, freed-up, crazy love. They rocked my world.

Our Headmaster scheduled transportation with the staff in order for me to avoid walking in the cold weather. My frequently inflamed right knee interfered with my daily capacity to endure our cold outdoors from October to May. I walked well all of September and most of October. Then, my facial expressions must have revealed some agony in my 20+ minute walk to school with an aching right knee. I planned to either hire a driver or rent a car. Before I could explore either option, my Headmaster and the staff once again presented to me my punched card: "problem solved, next issue please." I wondered if God allowed such unrelenting kindness because I would be exiting this world soon. I know how to love lavishly and care deeply. Receiving the same often feels unsettling. I stood amazed at the gracious kindnesses in the welcoming village of Torokszentmiklos that persisted from September 1, 2019 to June 15, 2020.

Celebrations at our school with and without our students included special acknowledgment of my presence and contributions to our school. My expressions of gratitude rather stunned the cultural norms of my Hungarian family. I laughed and educated them on my African-American cultural and southern USA geographic background. Their warm, gracious, and welcoming acceptance of me lifted my weary "hard to be black in America" soul.

The students in our primary school had not experienced an up close and personal relationship with a brown skinned person. Their intrigue intensified after I taught them the first song: "We are the World." The presence of a singing, brown-skinned, older, curly red-haired, hugging, loving English teacher from the USA dominated our building. With my theatrical background, I entertained the students and our teachers. In this way, the corridors, dining hall and other areas of the building found me greeting, smiling, and attracting the students' attention daily. What a rock star world for me.

The non-English speaking community in which I lived taught me to become the "Queen of Charades." The Hungarian language demands more attention than many other languages. Accurate pronunciation of the vocabulary allows you not to confuse the native speakers. Alas, I bowed to the Spanish language that surfaced often in my speech. I then decided to concentrate on my teaching strengths to navigate through my non-English speaking community. What a privilege to walk among these easy going, curious Hungarians sometimes stretching their necks dangerously while pedaling, through the neighborhood. I waved at everyone and even greeted them with smiles hoping, trusting to be neighborly, making new friends. That's exactly what happened. I made friends with a lovely English speaking young woman, an author, a model, and a nail technician named Sue Polgar. In her fun manicure shop, Sue provided excellent care and fellowship. She introduced me to two of her non-English speaking friends and we continue to communicate as of the writing of this manuscript. What an unbelievable opportunity to experience love through gift giving, non-verbal communication around snacks, pizza, tea and pastries, nature walking and visiting each other's homes.

Every Sunday, riding the train from Torokszentmiklos to my church in Budapest thrilled me. On Sundays, I leaped from my bed to make that 7:54 am train. It took a 1 hour 39 minute train ride, a 10 minute tram ride and a 15 minute Metro subway ride to get to my 10:30 am service in Budapest. In Europe, riding the train allowed me time to listen to all of my traditional, sacred/gospel and spirituals as I gazed upon the landscape of Hungary reflecting upon aspects of both European and American history. I appreciated the efficiency of the European train service and the reasonably priced tickets. How I longed for such transportation experiences in the USA. Nonetheless, I took advantage of as many train rides as my schedule permitted. I canvassed a bit of Eastern Europe and pondered its history of transition from communism to democracy. I celebrated the ways in which simple glances from my fellow humans with whom I could share smiles, nods, hand waves in the absence of language skills.

I experienced the absolute most fulfilling love, peace, joy, and satisfaction in my teaching assignments with grades 1-8 during my tenure at Ferenc Kolcsey Primary School. I began with them on the first day of school with a gorgeous floral arrangement as a welcome gift to me. I remember thinking that this assignment would be quite challenging for this high school teacher. Indeed I usually prepared lessons that required much more language acquisition and conceptual skills than these primary students possessed. My colleagues patiently worked with me showing me such grace and dignity all along the way. Finally, in an AHA moment, after having observed the instructional strategies and methodologies of my colleagues, I found myself preparing appropriate lessons that students found accessible. In this way, with my theatrical and vocal training,I arrived at a place of effectiveness that comforted me. In Spite of my Hungarian language challenges, I won over the students with whom I worked with genuine love, hope, faith and joy. We hugged, loved, sang, and studied one another's teaching and learning styles until we synced them to our delight. In the corridors, the dining room, the auditorium, the gym and all around and about the school, these little love lumps beat a path to my arms because they were already in my heart.

Hungary, I am indebted to you. I healed in your land. I healed from the heartache of losing my house, which had been a happy home. I healed from the distress of no longer perhaps you added some twenty (20) years to my life. I experienced kindness in many regions of the world; you, however, surpassed them all with your unrelenting acts of tenderheartedness toward me. May you receive a 100-fold return on your investment in my life.

Celebration Church

"I am a WINNER!"

...But speaking the truth in love, may grow up into him in all things, which is the head, even Christ: From whom the whole body fitly joined together and compacted by that which every joint supplieth, according to the effectual working in the measure of every part, maketh increase of the body unto the edifying of itself in love. Ephesians 4:15-16—KJV

In 2002, a modern architectural design of a church edifice in Long Reach Village, situated neatly there in a cul-de-sac—adjacent to a high rise senior citizen residence—offered me both respite and yet another transformation experience. Upon arrival, I took a deep breath and walked into the lobby of the then home of Long Reach Church of God. The warm greeting by the ushers settled my trembling upper torso. I asked myself: "Why do I feel nervous?" I wondered why I felt conspicuous. I contemplated why I felt alone. Nonetheless, I entered the sanctuary anticipating a worship experience and a sermon that might answer some of my frequently asked questions of God regarding my ordination after graduating from seminary. Because I graduated in May 2000 from seminary, I anticipated becoming ordained soon after. I then expected an offer in the vocational ministry. I thought of myself as well suited for Christian education. I just needed to be identified by someone as the right fit for their Christian education goals.

Sometimes, I rehearsed how my idealism hindered me. Practically, I appreciated that at 55 years of age, female and single—my appeal might be curious to search committees in western churches. Perhaps ageism exceeds sexism and racism. Nonetheless, I thought of myself as a youthful, vibrant and committed woman with respectable and even colorful lived experiences, skills, credentials and above all—a teachable attitude—to offer to the organized church. So, I tiptoed behind the usher to the seat where she directed me. I sat down smiling at the people on my left and right. I anticipated a new day dawning in my post seminary Christian journey. My experiences at this beloved then Long Reach Church of God, now Celebration Church far exceeded my expectations. The leadership of then Bishop Robert Stanley Davis, Sr. affectionately known as "Bishop Bob" and then First Lady Doris K. Davis—after their ministry labors of some thirty years—resulted in the passing of the baton to their only son, then Lead Pastor Robert Stanley Davis, Jr. affectionately known as Pastor Robbie and our First Lady Robin Davis. Over my seventeen years there—though I remain connected virtually in 2022—the church evolved from a name change, refocus of church polity, revisiting of cell groups/small groups to their mission statement: "Helping People to Win in Life on the foundation of a personal relationship with Jesus Christ."

In 2002 to 2019, I witnessed up close and personal the evolution of the growth, the realization of the vision for ministry of Bishop Bob and Lady Doris to the establishment and relocation of Celebration Church under the now leadership of Bishop Robbie Davis. As a single, never married with Godchildren but not biological children, I lived vicariously through the "R" family. Bishop Robbie and his bride of several decades now parented seven children and in the past few years, they have welcomed several grandchildren. I loved their family naming process. All of the children's names begin with the letter "r" rooted in Christian attributes and family heritage, which piqued my curiosity. To observe the growth of this family and church blessed my soul. I thought of how this family of two parents and seven children gratified my own ideas about family. Because of my keen interest in the von Trapp family singers, I often likened this family unto them—a strong image of having 8 children who would become family singers with me and my siblings. When I learned of the von Trapp family landing in Vermont and having accommodations that reminded them of Austria, I visited the von Trapp Lodge in Stowe, Vermont. How joyful to view photos of the actual family.

Nonetheless, the "R" family reminded me so often of the von Trapp family. Bishop Robbie and his sisters, along with his mom and her twin, gifted musicians, choir directors and vocalists established a rich heritage of sacred music both in our church and in the National Association of the Church of God. Bishop Robbie's youngest sister is an acclaimed Opera singer. Accordingly, Bishop Robbie and Pastor Robin's home, filled with music, resulted in musician/arts daughters as well as athletic, academically gifted sons and daughters. Such a joy to observe their journeys. Living vicariously through them, I felt fortunate!

The Back Story

Interestingly, I never planned to leave Washington, DC. I loved having a Washington, DC address. I felt the energy as I realized that I lived in the center of one of the world's most recognizable capital cities. I loved living in DC as it is affectionately known. Even more, I embraced the fruitful relationships near to my heart at both Howard University and especially Third Street Church of God [TSCOG.] For nearly twenty years, I both belonged to and shared in ministry at TSCOG in Washington, DC. There, I learned, under the tutelage of Rev. Dr. Samuel George Hines, the biblical principles of forgiveness and reconciliation. Third Street offered cultural diversity, musical excellence, superb teaching and preaching, a well organized Christian education ministry, evangelism opportunities and noteworthy community outreach with a history of breakfast, worship and other services for the homeless. I saw myself there for a lifetime. The church recorded some 250 plus members. This afforded this "people person over the top personality" to fulfilling relationships as well as sharing among multiple families and many friends. I spent quality time with the Herbert and Connie Woods family, the Paris and Lorna McIntyre family, the Victor Sr. and Alice W. Phillps family, the Willie and Rozena Marshall family, the Bobby and Sandra Key family, the Wallace and Doris Sanders family, the Levolia Goolsby family to name a few. When I first joined, Third Street had two well attended, lively and noteworthy services. I often remained for both the 8:00 am and 11:00 am services, eager to enjoy my new friends—all of them.

The long established generational families that belonged to and shared their ministry gifts at Third Street from their birth to their death captivated me. Commitment and discipline, signatures of many of the TSCOG members, inspired me to follow the lead of these families and ministry leaders. After graduating from seminary, I returned to our TSCOG—often mentioned in church circles—Third Street Church of God known across the city and beyond for a significant homeless breakfast/worship ministry. I preached to the attendees on a few occasions. What a compelling experience.

My enthusiasm spiraled sometimes uncontrollably because while matriculating at PTS, I felt like Deborah, Ruth and Mary. That mountaintop experience in seminary obliterated the agony of a traumatic experience in the 1996-97 school year with DC Public Schools. I seem to chase good trouble and find too much evil! Nonetheless, Now, I thought of myself as a seminary trained mature woman, bringing an enriched musical background and new skills, an unrelenting commitment to prayer, insights into women's ministries and good success with a 4-day, student driven, unprecedented reconciliation and forgiveness conference—all of this more fully preparing me for vocational ministry. I felt equipped and eager to become an asset to my beloved TSCOG. In the words of my student athletes, I found myself "pumped up and ready to roll." To my absolute satisfaction, I became the 8 am morning service worship leader. I worked closely with the musician, Madame Wanda Zambrana, with whom I enjoyed a sister girl friendship. Working closely with Wanda energized both of us. We met regularly and engaged one another joyfully examining the worship tasks, the sermonic themes and the appropriate music to enhance the entire worship experience. Though this voluntary ministry assignment blessed me, I trusted God and the leadership of TSCOG for direction toward vocational ministry.

After a little while at my cherished TSCOG, I realized that some missteps on my part resulted in a breach with our leadership. Wow, how could I manage to come from the PTS mountaintop experience to the poor judgment call at our church that resulted in a move to both a different church and a different city in the area. Nonetheless, after a few intense conferences with our esteemed pastor, who received nationwide respect, I needed to go forth. My relocation eventually allowed for "dual citizenship." Such a term, introduced to me by the gift to our music ministry in the person of Brother Franklin DeLaine, eased my sense of failure at TSCOG. Brother DeLaine, the resident sage, always refreshed me with his grace-filled words. When I shared with him and the leadership that I now would become a "best friend" to Third Street though I must take my leave, both he and the leadership accepted my decision. How difficult it is to depart from regular attendance and intimate contact with this stellar group of fellow laborers in the kingdom of God. How frustrating to make a judgment called that resulted in a vote of no confidence for my ordination. How grateful to God to get on the other side of that experience and to remain committed forever to the TSCOG family and leadership. Yet another example of God's perfect love poured into me, allowing his extravagant evidence to boost my confidence in remaining connected to my Third Street family. I continue to speak of this congregation as pivotal in my transformation process.

Secure at Celebration

My ministry tasks at Long Reach/Celebration began when I realized how fortunate for me that Bishop Bob adopted me as another one of his spiritual daughters. He assigned me straightaway to both his then Associate Pastor Suzanne Haley and to Cell/Small Group Leader Barbara Lewis. Pastor Suzanne counseled, encouraged and assisted me in preparing for the ordination process. Barbara Lewis, our small group leader, my anchor at Celebration Church, along with Connie Phillips, our small group hostess both taught me more about selflessness. Their commitment to serve inspired me to higher heights. Both [Deacon] Barbara Lewis [deceased] and Pastor Gloria Adams worked closely with me encouraging my vision for ministry, supporting my spiritual disciplines, inspiring my teaching and writing and overall caring for me as a sister and colleague in ministry. My dear readers, this chapter would expand for many more pages if only I could share with you the complete joy of sisterhood and community in Christ. I witnessed victory, transformation, deliverance, healing and abiding love in this small group. The painful loss of Gail Allen and Barbara Lewis sometimes haunts me, but only when I fail to rejoice knowing that I will see them again in eternal life with Christ. These women—Connie Phillips, Leah Taylor, Jean Parker, Toni Killings, Jocelyn Turner, Geralyn Boone, Earnestine Thomas, Gail Allen [deceased] Evelyn Jones, Lawanya Barfield, [her young son, Chris,] Melva Robinson, Wanda Telfair each in her unique way left an indelible impression on my transformation process. Our gatherings offered food, fun, fellowship and feasting on the word of God. We laughed, loved, labored and lingered with one another over several years. Their unrelenting support of my missions activities and my teaching ministry offered life extending energy to me.

Actually, this chapter would extend to several more pages if I were to acquaint readers with the many persons that God used to strengthen me all along the way. No monetary contribution pays for humans who give themselves entirely to another human to nurture them on their journey. In our small group, under the leadership of Deacon Barbara Lewis and Hostess Connie Phillips, I joined force with Leah Taylor, Jean Parker, Toni Killings, Jocelyn Turner, Geralyn Boone, Earnestine Thomas, Gail Allen [deceased] Evelyn Jones, Lawanya Barfield, Marva Robinson, and Wanda Telfair. Occasionally, Toni Johns Blount could join us. We learned to build one another up in the Lord. We understood from our leader and hostess what immeasurable selflessness looks like, sounds like, feels like. We witnessed how shared space, comforting outreach, and life-sacrificing time on task with one another transforms lives. Without fail, we saw the greatest results from this behavior. We see it as others respond affirmatively and go forth giving as life has been given to them. I believe in God and in small group/community ministry. This is where we see Christ at work within us. Each woman in my small group and in my two additional small group settings with women, left her fingerprint upon my transformation process. Their unrelenting support of my missions activities and my teaching ministry offered life extending energy to me. My small group with the women's prayer breakfast planning committee enriched my strong sense of purpose. We respected the leadership of Rosetta Thompson, Linda McEwen, Denys Wright-Thisedale, Chrystal Winters, Darlene Bright, Toni Johns Blount, Jackie Palmer and and a few others of us who spent quality time together laughing, laboring, learning and lingering around the ministry tasks to share a prayer breakfast that enhanced our sisterhood.

I invested hundreds of hours in a small group ministry with women. I shared faithfully with the prayer ministry named Adam's Portion where under the tutelage of Pastor Gloria Adams, participants learned more of the depth, breath, power and authority of God's word to critically effect change in one's circumstances. We gathered faithfully on Monday evenings, enjoyed light refreshments and listened attentively to the anointed teaching of this gifted disciple of Christ. Our interactions among each other gave new meaning to the scripture "iron sharpens iron." We cried, prayed, shared, cared, celebrated one another's journeys, joys and sorrows. We supported one another through the seasons of our lives. I watched their children come of age, graduate from high school, college, marry and begin their families. What a privilege for me!

Pastor Kevin Johnson added his leadership skills, administrative tasks and wealth of knowledge to the Christian education ministry titled WIN Institute. The long standing Christian education ministry fully supported and directed over the years by Pastor Ernie Davis, later expanded by Ministers Damus and Ruthie Fortune emphasized the church's mission and the vision of both Bishop Bob and Pastor Robbie. I admired the teaching and training energy His 3-inch binder used to share with our voluntary staff inspired content excellence. Our training as we offered, taught, trained others in Christian education ministry. Our curriculum provided a wide array of courses. Each course stimulated growth and inspired maturity for those who wish to delve more deeply into the scriptures, examine practical application of the scriptures, enhance their prayer life.

The Winning Women of Celebration Church [WWCC] alternate retreat and conference planning committee intensified my prayer life. Pastor Robin offered me the position of Chaplain for the committee. Fully satisfied with my sense of purpose, I prepared diligently prayers that I trusted would increase our faith in God and confidence in one another. I had spent several decades previously in prayer ministries during my first two Church of God experiences. I embraced the prayer ministry profoundly important to my life's mission. I resonated with the one-word themes [twice two word themes] that then Lady Robin generally chose from specific scripture references. As a tribute to Pastor Robin and our entire WWCC Ministry the following is my incorporation of these themes [italicized] along my Christian journey:

I finally believed that I can be "FREE" from the missteps that resulted in my late bloomer achievements. How refreshing to "LAUGH" at my mistakes and dust myself off, beginning afresh with greater confidence in the joy of being "CLOSE" to my sisters in growth and development. How comforting to "BREATHE" as we breeze through the demanding tasks of preparing for retreat or conference activities with which and to which women could resonate, respect and respond. I felt "CLOSE" to God working in community with my sisters in our WWCC. I remember embracing a heartfelt teaching in seminary by a noteworthy theologian that said: "If it is not community, Christ is not in it." Through thorny moments as we met tight deadlines and budgetary constraints, I prayed the most, finding myself absolutely one of our "SHE'S INTENTIONAL" sisters—unwilling to shrink back in doubt that God would not work out the most arduous tasks for us. Perhaps you could call me "UNSTOPPABLE" as I and my committee of devout sister girls prayed in season and out. If I named them here and failed to name all of them, I would serve no good purpose. They know who they were and who they are to me and our prayer ministry "FOREVER." Clearly, we WWCC committed to a "RIGHT NOW" posture during all times but perhaps even more so during the painful deaths of our fellow chaplain, Rev. Ridia Reid, former WWCC presenters like my discipler Deacon Barbara Lewis, and several other dear sisters. Thank God that we will see them again on the other side. Elder Sondra Jackson, Pastor Robin and all of the WWCC, please know that along my spiritual journey, you left your fingerprints on my heart, now such fingerprints are reinforced by the benefit of this reflection.

My parents taught their children by precept and example to aim high and finish every achievement with excellence. They discouraged mediocrity so much so that I thought it must be sinfully wicked to ever even think of settling for mediocrity. My dad became a humble porter, after the loss of his right hand in an automobile accident. He cleaned the lodge where he worked as if Jesus and the disciples would be meeting there—amazing—the detailed cleaning that he did every day. My brothers asked why? How could Daddy put that kind of effort into a place where they did all kinds of socializing and shared beverages—none of which necessarily honored the word of God to which my Daddy gave his life. Daddy taught us to work beyond mediocrity in all circumstances whether you agree with the situation or not.

In this way, I saw evidence of excellence—not perfection—all along the way at Celebration Church. I understand that perfection is in God alone. We humans strive to do things excellently to honor God. I believe that striving for perfection opens the door to prideful behavior. The scripture is clear: pride goes before destruction. I appreciated the high standards that then Pastor Robbie and now Bishop Robbie held and hold for his preaching ministers, his staff, his vision for ministry, his parenting, his family, his followers and himself. I got on board with the attitude of excellence and worked earnestly to prepare my workshops, sermons, prayers, and bathroom duties. Aha, perhaps many readers will wonder what role I played in bathroom duty. I bought accessories to enhance the presentation of the women's bathroom located in the lobby of our Foreland Garth building. I prepared scriptures, printed them on lovely, colorful stock paper, laminated them and placed them on the doors in the women's bathroom. I did bathroom detail duty many Sundays—tidying up the sinks, floors, individual commodes, and the area immediately outside the door of the ladies room. I needed to support Brother Paul Haley when keeping our facility with supplies was a part of his Sunday duty and then Brother John Blount when that task was a part of his Sunday duty. I wanted to remind myself every Sunday for many months that no task was beneath me. I wanted to honor the excellence of my Daddy as a janitor. I, too, with my three Master's degrees and a fourth Master's degree hanging in the balance, needed to be reminded of excellence in the tidying up of the women's bathroom. In all things—excellence. Yes.

Well excellence, high achievement, advancing beyond mediocrity always crashes into adversity. What do I mean by this? As soon as you decide to become excellent and to model it for your peers, circumstances seem to demand that you stay with that idea even when things go a whole different way. Though both Bishop Bob and Pastor Robbie, Pastor Larry as well as other leaders at Celebration affirmed me, I struggled to establish myself in vocational ministry. In the scriptures, the disciples encountered a blind man. In summary, they asked Jesus who sinned that this man was born blind. Jesus shared with them neither the man nor his parents sinned but that this blind condition allowed the works of God to be manifested in this man's life. I studied that scripture in John 9. I then owned it as one of my testimonies. Neither I nor my parents sinned that my seminary training, ordination, vision for ministry did unfold according to the ideas in my mind. In a conversation with Pastor Larry in the summer of 2019, I lamented with him the things that were and the things that were not with regard to my expectations for ministry. In wise counsel, he said a few things that I needed to hear. What he said that I wrestled with for some weeks to come was simply: "The will of God", "right," he interjected, "but the will of God." "CarolAnn," he repeated, "the will of God." From those fitly spoken words, I journeyed to Hungary with unrelenting support from Celebration Church and our extended family. I found myself believing that I, similar to the man in John 9, had not sinned that my ministry seemingly faded; but that the works of God must be manifested in this woman's life. I believed that. Those words, "the will of God" comforted me for many weeks to come and even now.

Respectfully, I reserve the right to celebrate my unsung heroes in the Celebration family: prayer warriors like Chaplain Gerald Washington, Elder Kenneth Cooper, wise counselors like Pastor Mike Edwards, Deacon Linda McEwen, Mother Essie Powell, Graphic Artist Carmelle Scott…so many others who refresh you in a snatched conversation with them. As we listen to one another, we learn, we glean, we grow! I love fighting to overcome an average performance. I love the examples my parents taught me. I love that God is our help and will help us to achieve our goals even in the midst of the most challenging circumstances. Mom loved to say to us: "No matter who tells you that you can't do it or that it can't be done, that person is not GOD. Let God show you and others that you CAN do it and that it CAN be done.

Blessings beloved Celebration Church. I am a transformed creature and you participated critically in this process. In fact, your total impact along with that of others along my life's journey remains to be revealed. Bishop Robbie, Pastor Robin and the entire Celebration United families: Go forth and WIN in life intentionally with Jesus Christ as our leader, our guide and our keeper. Indeed we remain unstoppable. To God be the glory.

About the Author

CarolAnn North is a seminary-trained and ordained minister and missionary. After several years on the mission field as well as thirty years of inner-city teaching and ministry experience, CarolAnn relocated from Columbia, Maryland, to her native home in San Antonio, Texas. Currently she continues writing inspirational nonfiction and music as well as historical poetry.